The American Prospect

The American Prospect

☆ ☆

Insights into Our Next 100 Years

EDITED BY
Henry F. Thoma

HOUGHTON MIFFLIN COMPANY
BOSTON 1977

Library of Congress Cataloging in Publication Data
Main entry under title:
The American prospect.
1. United States — Civilization — 1970–
— Addresses, essays, lectures.   I. Thoma, Henry F.
E169.12.A43   973.925   76-58904
ISBN 0-395-25354-3   ISBN 0-395-25405-1 pbk.

Printed in the United States of America

V 10 9 8 7 6 5 4 3 2 1

Preface

NEW ENGLAND is proud of its capacity to face adversity. It has
seen its clipper ships disappear over the horizon. It has
waved goodby to its farmers departing for the deep soil of the
Middle West. It has agonized over the textile and other manu-
facturers who have moved operations to a seemingly more
congenial South and West. None of these changes in commerce, agriculture, or manufacturing has been easy to face.
Yet by developing ingenuity and varied skills, New England
has survived and — in many ways — prospered.

The problems of survival in 1976 are not those of a region
but of a nation. It now appears that all America is obliged to
face situations both at home and abroad every bit as difficult
as those faced by New England in the past two centuries. The
character of many of these situations has been a central thread
of the Bicentennial Forums held in the fall of 1975 and the first
half of 1976.

The first series of Bicentennial Forums held in the winter
and spring of 1975 was published as *The American Experiment*.
The second series, included in this book, followed a format
similar to the first. Distinguished observers were invited to
present a formal address at late-afternoon meetings held in

Faneuil Hall and New England Life Hall. Questions from the audience were answered following each of these addresses. Subsequently, after a dinner at the Parkman House, fifteen to twenty special guests engaged the speaker in a more intensive and frequently far-ranging discussion of the issues raised in the afternoon.

By and large, the addresses and discussions in the first series of the Bicentennial Forums were retrospective, viewing the American Experiment in the light of 200 years of history. They stressed the origin and growth of our national institutions and beliefs, and how they gave form to what we have become.

. . . A judge sketched the source and development of The Rights of Man, showing how this great concept took shape in the minds of our Founding Fathers.

. . . A professor of history contrasted the role of institutions in the present day with those in being at the time of the War of Independence from Britain.

. . . A distinguished lady reviewed the rise and fall of totalitarianism in twentieth-century Europe and saw a tragic spillover into America's recent past.

. . . A congressman — famed for his role in the Nixon proceedings — examined the impeachment power and its role in holding elected officials accountable.

. . . A former mayor of our largest city expressed the view that Americans may no longer be champions of freedom and individual rights, but "cautious and silent, resistant to change."

In contrast — and as is most fitting — the speakers in the second series of the Bicentennial Forums addressed The American Prospect. They focused less on history and forces that shaped our national development and more on problems we must somehow resolve in the years ahead. Thus in this volume are reports by

. . . A distinguished historian of the law, who reconsidered the concepts of unity and diversity in our culture today, and considered how the apparent conflict between the ideals of equality and the pursuit of excellence may be treated.

. . . An economist, who outlined a bold plan for transforming the ownership of capital from a relative few to a majority of our citizens.

. . . The Managing Director of the British Broadcasting System, who stressed the vital role of the media in our times, and candidly commented on the shortcomings of American television.

. . . A senator and candidate for the presidency in 1972, who felt that imbalances in the present tax structure, large concentrations of economic power, and the giant military-industrial complex would continue to need controls in the years ahead.

. . . A recent ambassador to the United Nations, and now senator from New York, who expressed his concern with the pervasive unhappiness in large elements of the population, and the reduced efforts of government analysts to discover the roots of this unease.

. . . The executive director of the National Urban League, who deplored the position of blacks and other minorities, yet saw the possibility of further improvements.

. . . A distinguished Boston attorney, who discussed the need for agreement on the philosophy underlying our government and the "desperate prospect" of its survival if "its soul or animating principle ebbs away."

All these observers were realistic, yet none ended on a note of despair. If anything, they can be read as seeing in America a new awakening, a clearer consciousness of our role in the world, and the first steps toward greater maturity. If we conclude that technological advance and material plenty are not the only measures of progress, if we acknowledge that our methods do not necessarily apply to all the nations of the world, and if we work openly to improve our own society —

then perhaps we can attain the respect and understanding we have always sought for American principles in the rest of the world.

To the degree that these Bicentennial Forums show ways toward such growth and maturity, they may prove more valuable to others than to the participants. Coming at a time when the nation was forced to acknowledge its limits in policing the world and grievous shortcomings in its own governance, they may be of use in its search for the role it will play in the decades ahead.

As was indicated in *The American Experiment*, the Bicentennial Forums were jointly sponsored by New England Mutual Life Insurance Company, the Parkman Center for Urban Affairs, the city's research and conference center, and Boston 200, the city's Bicentennial Agency. The sponsors are especially grateful to Howard W. Johnson, chairman of the Program Advisory Committee, whose assistance in putting the series together was invaluable; to Mayor Kevin H. White for his enthusiastic endorsement and active participation; to Katherine D. Kane, head of Boston 200 — and now deputy mayor — and her successor, Harron Ellenson; to David Rosenbloom, director of the Parkman Center during much of the period covered by the Forums; and to Gordon D. MacKay, David V. Lustig, and Karen Mazo of New England Life, who handled most of the arrangements.

We are especially grateful to Houghton Mifflin Company which, by publishing both series of Forums, has made a signal contribution to the Bicentennial celebrations. Mr. Henry F. Thoma — a recently retired member of that firm — returned to active service expressly for the purpose of editing these publications with his own special style and skill.

It is our hope that the Bicentennial Forums will not only reflect a significant examination of contemporary issues in American life, but that they may also constitute a chapter in contemporary history. Many insights were expressed concerning political, economic, and social problems that may be expected to be with us for many years. If these insights play a part in the solution of these problems, the Forums will have accomplished their prime objective.

ABRAM T. COLLIER
Chairman of the Board
New England Mutual
Life Insurance Company

Contents

A Note on the Bicentennial Forums

THIS "PROGRAM ADVISORY COMMITTEE" met just once in formal session, on July 24, 1974, but it was a most productive encounter indeed. A majority of the Committee was in attendance, and the late-afternoon session lasted well into the evening.

While a variety of formats, schedules, and substantive options was freely discussed, the Committee's deliberations led it to the following recommendations:

. . . the Forums were to be based on fundamental principles and contradictions, such as the conflict between freedom and responsibility or the problem of executive versus legislative balance in government.

. . . Speakers were to be selected primarily for their intellectual prowess and experience in dealing with the practical problems which result from the contradictions in societal values.

. . . An opportunity was to be provided for a thorough critique of speakers' views through the vehicle of a lengthy discussion with their peers in the Boston area.

. . . Publication of the Forums and follow-up discussions were to be sought to provide a permanent record of the project of real value to both students and laymen, and electronic dissemination through radio and television to the general public was to be encouraged.

Houghton Mifflin Company agreed to participate through the publication of a two-volume set of books on the Forums (of which this work is the second). And Boston's WBUR-FM and the National Public Radio Network produced a series of coast-to-coast broadcast specials.

Throughout the tenure of the Forums in 1975 and 1976, members of the Committee continued to play an important role as participants in and constructive critics of our examination of the American Experiment. For the record, and to ensure that their contribution to Boston's reflection on the state of the nation receives due recognition, I should like to note the names of those who served on the Committee.

Dr. Harold Amos, professor of bacteriology and immunology, Harvard Medical School; Daniel Bell, professor of sociology, Harvard University; David M. French, department of community medicine, Boston University School of Medicine; Honorable Bill E. Frenzel, Member of the House of Representatives from Minnesota; General James M. Gavin, chairman of the board, Arthur D. Little, Inc.; Honorable Margaret M. Heckler, Member of the House of Representatives from Massachusetts; Richard D. Hill, chairman, First National Bank of Boston; Elliot Klitzman, business agent, Joint Board of the International Ladies Garment Workers Union; Reverend J. Donald Monan, S.J., president, Boston College; Frank E. Morris, president, Federal Reserve Bank of Boston; Art Naparstek, director, National Center for Urban Ethnic Affairs; Honorable David R. Obey, Member of the House of Representatives from Wisconsin; Honorable Thomas P. O'Neill, Jr., majority leader of the House of Representatives from Massachusetts; Nan S. Robinson, vice president for planning, University of Massachusetts; Paul A. Samuelson, professor of economics, Massachusetts Institute of Technology; Sam Bass Warner, Jr., professor of history, Boston University; Paul N. Ylvisaker, dean, Harvard Graduate School for Education; and ex officio, Abram T. Collier, chairman, New England Mutual Life Insurance Company; Katherine D. Kane, deputy mayor and (then) director, Mayor's Office of the Boston Bicentennial; Honorable Kevin H. White, Mayor of Boston; and Henry Steele Commager, the historian.

HOWARD W. JOHNSON
Chairman of the Corporation,
Massachusetts Institute of Technology
Chairman Program Advisory Committee,
Bicentennial Forums

1

Unity and Diversity — Changing Meanings

PAUL FREUND

The second series of the Bicentennial Forums was inaugurated at New England Life Hall on a fine October afternoon with an address by one of the nation's leading scholars of law and the judicial system. To an eager audience, many of whom remembered stirring moments from the first Forums series, he spoke fittingly of two delicate balances essential to our brand of democracy — that between unity and diversity and that between equality and the pursuit of excellence. He thus looked back to the historic struggles, both legal and social, out of which these precarious balances were wrung, and forward to the eternal effort necessary to maintain and improve them against the forces of selfishness, indifference, and ignorance. Here was a rare view of the legal mind at its best — historian, philosopher, and teacher all at once.

Paul Freund began his law career as clerk to Justice Louis Brandeis in 1932 and 1933, spent the next eight years in the Treasury Department and the Solicitor General's Office, and has been a member of the Harvard Law School faculty since 1939. He was Pitt Professor of American History and Institutions at Cambridge University in 1957 and 1958, holds honorary degrees from seventeen colleges and universities, and is now Carl M. Loeb University Professor. He is the author of many articles and a number of books, among them The Supreme Court of the United States, On

1

Law and Justice, Cases on Constitutional Law, *and (in preparation)* History of the Supreme Court.

WHEN WE LOOK ABROAD today and watch the painful struggle to achieve some kind of unity in diverse parts of the globe — in Western Europe, not to speak of Europe as a whole, in Africa, in the Middle East — we have fresh reason to marvel at the "miracle in Philadelphia" in 1787. Bringing political union out of thirteen scattered populations was an achievement gained against great odds. The cleavages among the states were enormous: different religious establishments in different states, slaveholding versus free labor, seaport states levying tribute through customs duties on imports destined for sister states, and above all, ignorance of one another imposed by distances. Madison wrote frankly, "Of the People of Georgia I know as little as of those of Kamkatska." Not only ignorance but provincial pride: William Maclay, a peppery yeoman and classicist who represented Pennsylvania in the first Senate of the United States, wrote in his diary: "We Pennsylvanians act as if we believed that God made of one blood all families of the earth; but the Eastern people seem to think that he made none but New England folk. It is strange that men born and educated under republican forms of government should be so contracted on the subject of general philanthropy. In Pennsylvania, used as we are to the reception and adoption of strangers, we receive no class of men with such diffidence as the Eastern people. They really have the worst characters of any people who offer themselves for citizens. Yet these are the men who affect the greatest fear of being contaminated with foreign manners, customs, or vices. Perhaps it is with justice that they fear an adoption of any of the latter, for they surely have enough already."

How then can we explain the consensus that emerged after three arduous months in the summer of 1787? There were, I suggest, four conditions that underlay the great compromises reached by the Constitutional Convention. First, a sense of urgency, lest the states succumb to the anarchy of endless reprisals and become the laughingstock of their European friends and foes. Second, the careful preparatory work that enabled the delegates to focus on concrete proposals. Third, a spirit of accommodation, which was supported by, fourth, the absolute secrecy of the proceedings. I sometimes think that if there had been investigative journalists hovering about the corridors gathering material for their daily columns (the daily calumnists, Chief Justice Hughes called them), there might well not have been a Constitution. The most thorough record of the proceedings, Madison's Notes, was not published until fifty years had passed. Of course the Constitution itself was debated thoroughly in the state ratifying conventions; it was an open covenant secretly arrived at.

For all its brilliance in achieving the unity of a federation, the Constitution would not have produced real nationhood without the magisterial vision of a jurist like John Marshall. The unity of a common market — freedom from economic parochialism — depended on his encompassing view of the economic powers of Congress, the limits placed on state authority over commerce that concerned more states than one, and the role of the national judiciary in turning back states' encroachments. We tend to forget that economic and juridical unity were bitter fighting issues, such that when the Supreme Court decided that it could review the decisions of state courts, the redoubtable Chief Justice Roane of Virginia was moved to exclaim, "A most monstrous and unexampled decision. It can only be accounted for by that love of power which all history informs us infects and corrupts all who possess it, and from which even the upright and eminent judges are not exempt . . . (It is the) zenith of despotic power." "The career of the High Court must be stopped or the liberties of our country are annihilated."

Justice Holmes spoke justly of Marshall's achievement.

"When we celebrate Marshall," he said, "we celebrate at the same time and indivisibly the inevitable fact that the oneness of the nation and the supremacy of the national Constitution were declared to govern the dealings of man with man by the judgments and decrees of the most august of courts." The oneness of the nation — yes, the physical and economic and juridical unity of the nation in matters of national concern. But the moral unity of the nation remained to be secured, so far as law can secure it. The post–Civil War constitutional amendments furnished the framework for national standards of due process and equal protection of the laws — a framework that became a true structure a hundred years after the Civil War, with the civil-rights legislation of the 1960s and the decisions of the Supreme Court during the last several decades.

The ideal of unity, however, has its limits. Just as the future biological welfare of the human race depends on a diversity of genetic traits, so the vitality of the nation depends on the cultural diversity of its people. "One out of many" is our official motto: "E pluribus unum." Better, perhaps, would be the motto "One together with many": "Cum pluribus unum." There was a time when the ideal of unity found its model in the melting pot; now we take as the model the symphony orchestra, its various choirs distinct and yet interfused.

Our values have gone awry when economic and juridical unity is eroded — when there are regional pockets of poverty and a checkerboard pattern of capital punishment across the land — and at the same time cultural unity advances through conformity — through the imitative pattern of the television network programs, the indistinguishable patterns of attire, the endless replicas of Main Street beside the endless stretches of superhighway. After two hundred years we need to reexamine the perpetual problem of the One and the Many, to see whether we have become many when we should be one, and one when we ought to be many.

When we turn from the theme of unity to that of equality, we have to confess that the record has been spotty. To be sure, the Declaration of Independence proclaimed that all men are created equal — not, of course, in physical or mental or material endowments, but in intrinsic worth in their common humanity, in their fundamental rights as members of the civil society. The concept of equality was not carried into the Constitution, and not until 1868, with the adoption of the Fourteenth Amendment, was there a formal guarantee of equal protection of the laws.

Even that guarantee was not thought to embrace women, least of all married women. When a well-qualified woman lawyer, Myra Bradwell of Chicago, sought admission to practice before the Supreme Court of the United States in 1872, she was politely but firmly turned away. Justice Bradley, generally a sagacious judge content to find his law in mundane sources, this time appealed to higher authority. "The paramount mission and destiny of women," he said, "are to fulfill the noble and benign offices of wife and mother. This is the law of the Creator." Even the counsel who represented Ms. Bradwell in the Supreme Court was guarded in his claims. He made it clear that he was not advocating female suffrage, "which," he said, "it is assumed, would overthrow Christianity, defeat the ends of modern civilization, and upturn the world." It is difficult to distinguish irony and humorlessness on this highly charged issue. The stereotype of woman conveniently overlooked the formidable Abigail Adams, who held her own in serious correspondence with her husband's successor, Thomas Jefferson, on basic constitutional issues. But that, of course, took place in a primitive, unsophisticated age. Can anyone imagine, today, a similar correspondence between, say, President Ford and the widow of President Kennedy?

I should add, as an historic footnote, that Congress intervened on behalf of the eligibility of women to become

5

members of the Supreme Court bar, and in 1879 the first woman attorney was admitted. Perhaps on the centennial of that occasion we shall see a woman seated not at the bar but on the bench.

Divine authority was found not merely for the subordination of women. It helped to assuage as well guilt feelings over the subjection of blacks. What is more surprising is that Holy Writ was cited to warn against the subversive influence of immigrants. Another member of the Supreme Court, Justice Brewer of Kansas, was addressing the New York State Bar Association at its annual meeting in 1893, two years before the federal income tax was held unconstitutional. The tone of the address is sufficiently indicated by this short passage: " 'To him that hath shall be given', is the voice of Scripture. 'From him that hath shall be taken,' is the watchword of a not inconsiderable and, owing to the influx of foreign voters, a growing portion of our population." Perhaps it was too early to perceive that second-generation immigrants tend, if anything, to become fierce supporters of the status quo.

How can stereotypes be combated? Through closer acquaintance and association, the answer runs. And yet association and acquaintance are the very things that stereotype images generally prevent. At the time of the troubles in Little Rock over school desegregation in 1957, a novel experiment was tried. A small group of school children, white and black, were invited to participate in an unrehearsed radio program, during which they spoke their minds; and in the course of that discussion the white pupils actually lost their prejudices. The listeners had the rare experience of hearing the process of conversion. The discussion was reproduced in the *New York Times* of October 20, 1957, and I suggest that on the anniversary of that event the transcript be reprinted. It ended with the following exchanges:

> MINNIJEAN (a black pupil): . . . do you know anything about me, or is it just what your mother had told you about Negroes? . . .

MRS. RICKETTS (moderator): . . . Have you ever really made an effort to try to find out what they're like?

KAY: Not until today.

SAMMY: Not until today.

MRS. RICKETTS: And what do you think about it after today?

KAY: Well, you know that my parents and a lot of the other students and their parents think that the Negroes aren't equal to us. But — I don't know. It seems like they are, to me.

SAMMY: These people are — we'll have to admit that.

ERNEST: I think like we're doing today, discussing our different views . . . if the people of Little Rock would get together I believe they would find out a different story — and try to discuss the thing instead of getting out into the street and kicking people and calling names . . .

KAY: I think that if our friends had been getting in this discussion today, I think that maybe some of them — not all of them — in time, they would change their mind. But probably some of them would change their mind today.

SAMMY: I know now that it isn't bad as I thought it was — after we got together and discussed it . . .

MRS. RICKETTS : Let's see. Is there anything, finally, we want to say that we have to say now?

KAY: [Sammy and I] both came down here today with our mind set on it [that] we weren't going to change our mind that we were fully against integration. But I know now that we're going to change our mind.

MRS. RICKETTS: What do your parents say to that?

KAY: I think I'm going to have a long talk with my parents.

In the fall of 1957 I was in England and was asked to speak on Little Rock. In the course of my remarks I quoted the foregoing passage, and added, "One can hope that in this colloquy there speaks, unaffected and uncoerced, the voice of the future." Now, eighteen years later, one still must hope. More dialogues like that one could help.

As the ideal of unity would be sterile without diversity, the ideal of equality would be impoverishing were it not accompanied by the pursuit of excellence. At bottom, equality of opportunity and excellence are not in conflict; they are mutually reinforcing. For the wellsprings of excellence need to be

7

sought over a wide social terrain. The point is, not that there is an essential conflict, but rather that in our preoccupation with the painful struggle toward equality we not slacken in our search for excellence and its cultivation. The major advances in scientific and social thought as well will come from the exceptionally gifted, and there is no reason for apology, and every reason for pride, in discovering exceptional gifts and providing a suitably challenging educational environment for their flowering. After all, we cannot afford to rely on an influx of genius through exiles from abroad.

Amid the tensions between unity and diversity, between equality and excellence, there is finally the need for a sense of amity, of community. The conditions for achieving community seem to me to be threefold: economic, intellectual, and spiritual.

One need not be an economic determinist to appreciate the civilizing and cohesive effect of a diffused prosperity. Some years ago the mayor of Atlanta was fond of describing the racial situation there by saying "Atlanta is too busy to hate." Certainly a scarcity of work and competition for the places above the poverty level are prime exacerbators of disunity. I am aware that revolutions have typically occurred not at the nadir of the degradation of the lower classes but at a point when their plight is somewhat improved. Nevertheless, in a country where material success is held out as the prime indicator of personal worth, and where at the same time the doors toward that goal appear to be hopelessly closed, conditions are ripe, if not for revolution, as least for crime and bitter disunion.

On the intellectual level, a sense of community requires perspective, the placing of differences in the context of resemblances, a perspective that questions whether such disputes as history has witnessed between salvation by grace and salvation by works really justified the loss of a single life or a single friend. A universality of vision is the surest appeal to the sense of community. Witness the response, transcending race or creed or nation, to the simple humanity of a Gandhi, a Martin Luther King, or a Pope John.

And finally, on the spiritual level, there is the deepest ground for community. Thomas Hobbes remarked that the most fundamental equality of human beings is their equal vulnerability while asleep. At least of comparable significance is the equality of human ignorance covering the ultimate questions of existence — whence, and why, and whither. And so in the end the most telling ground for community is a decent humility.

Questions and Discussion

The generous discussion period that followed Professor Freund's address brought out a number of questions reflecting the concerns of the audience. Many of these were about busing and desegregation, and Freund made it clear that he stood solidly in favor of carrying out the law. Several persons asked whether the Constitution could provide for economic change extensive enough to make possible large public expenditure, and again the answer was an unqualified yes.

But perhaps the most thoughtful question asked from the floor — and it came up in a number of ways — had to do with the pursuit of excellence and the ideal of equality. How can these two *not* be in conflict? Can there be equality in the pursuit of excellence when there are such wide discrepancies in economic standing? If there is to be equal opportunity for all, is not the idea of excellence irrelevant? How can we correct the common misconception that material success is the prime indicator of personal worth? Some found it hard to resolve a conflict between the long-cherished ideal of equality — had we not even come to believe that everyone should go to col-

9

lege? — and this disquieting notion that something more was
needed than just being given a chance.

The talk continued that evening among a group of invited
guests after dinner at the Parkman House, one of Boston's old
mansions, in the shadow of the State House near the crest of
Beacon Hill. Built in 1824 close to the site of John Hancock's
residence and overlooking Boston Common, it remained in the
Parkman family — whose best-known member was the historian Francis Parkman — until 1908, when it was given to the
city. In 1973 it was splendidly restored as a guesthouse for distinguished visitors, and parts of it were converted into an
urban conference center.

In addition to the afternoon speaker, the evening panel included the former head of the Parkman Center, the deputy
mayor of Boston, a historian, a publisher, and several members
of the Massachusetts bar — a distinguished judge, several attorneys in private practice, and two in the court system, one
an eloquent young female public defender.

The discussion took off from several matters touched on in
Professor Freund's address. The first of these was economic
planning, which some thought might become necessary if the
energy crisis became really severe. Professor Freund thought
all-out economic planning could be accommodated by the
present system without a constitutional amendment, but that
it would be very hard work to put over. He pointed out that
while some economists are pushing hard for some kind of national economic planning council with computers and centralized records — all to be strictly informational, to give business more data for use in its own planning — most business
leaders fear that such an agency could all too easily become an
entering wedge for a socialized economy. And if we should
come to that we would be facing a problem no country has yet
solved — how to control the controllers, how to maintain an
acceptable measure of personal freedom — and still tell people
where they shall work and perhaps even how many children

they may have. So far we have controls over the stock market, but we don't tell people where to invest their money. The experience with limited planning in the Depression was not reassuring. Justice Brandeis used to say that the National Recovery Administration ought to be charged up to the Office of Education. If we sink into a deep enough depression we may have to go a long way in the direction of planning. But most people would rather stumble along and suffer than face that kind of control over their lives.

The whole question of computerized information and the invasion of privacy led to an expression of concern about how well lawyers and the law itself are functioning under the increased demands on them, and this led to the major discussion of the evening. Professor Freund began with a classic statement about the importance of law in society. He answered the complaint that ordinary daily justice is in trouble and needs help by saying that he could make similar complaints about dentistry and medicine — in short, that the professions generally in this country have probably not made themselves thoroughly available or had the greatest possible impact.

He then continued: "But when you speak of law in terms of what goes on in the courts, you're really talking about a small fragment of law, only the pathological side of it. The legal system is like the air we breathe, and the fact that we don't think of it that way indicates how well it is functioning. For example, you cash a check at a bank, and you don't give it another thought. But there's a very elaborate legal system which makes it possible for us to live on credit in this way. Again, the ordinary man says with assurance, 'Well, I'm safe. I've got it here in black and white.' In other words he's got somebody's name on a contract, and he depends on it without even consciously thinking about the power that lies behind that faith. Ordinarily the check clears and the contract binds because both parties act in accordance with the accepted body of law that controls such things. But every so often somebody

11

defaults or questions, and the matter has to go to court. Yet the system as a whole runs so smoothly that most people are scarcely aware that it exists at all. It is a substratum of practically everything we do, in ownership of property, rental of property, marriage, contracts, protection from superior force and chicanery, consumer problems, labeling, pure food laws, gun laws, and on and on.

"So when we condemn delays in the courts, we're talking about a very real but only a fractional part of law and order. The police courts and the magistrates' courts are of course the most congested. They are the most demeaning and generally sordid, and a lot of legal services ought to be made available in them that aren't for economic reasons. But something is being done about these problems. There is more legal aid than there used to be. Every defendant charged with a serious offense, even a serious misdemeanor, is entitled to private counsel, and appeals are abundant, perhaps too much so. If we wanted to cut off appeals, or to make them very expensive as they are in England, that would expedite justice a little. On the other hand, many people would feel that they hadn't gotten a fair deal that way because they hadn't got a review of the trial judge's decision.

"Actually," Professor Freund concluded, "I think the problem goes a lot deeper than the courts and the criminal law. Tougher decisions and longer sentences won't help; there are always other people ready to take the places of the dope peddlers and others who are convicted. It's the social and psychological mainstreams of crime that we aren't competent to deal with. It's easy to abuse the judge or the legal system, but for rehabilitation it seems to me that if anything our sentences are too long — longer than they are in Europe. So it's easier to condemn the judges than to say let's have more psychologists in prisons, let's have better living conditions, let's see that people get public works jobs instead of hanging around street corners, let's revive the youth conservation corps. In short, let's give people something to live for without the aid of LSD. But that takes a lot of thought, a lot of money, and a lot of manpower. And who's got any of these things?"

One aspect of delay and inefficiency in the court system was brought out by two panelists who were not members of the bar — one a historian and the other a publisher — both of whom had served long terms of jury duty. The principal complaint of both was that they were required to spend an enormous amount of time doing very little work. In the Suffolk County Superior Court jury pool, for example, several hundreds of men and women spend twenty days or so — a full month of working time — and during that period may actually sit on juries no more than three to five days. The rest of the time they have literally nothing to do, unless they bring their own work with them, and few can do that. Perhaps worse still, teachers, doctors, lawyers, and many other professional people are exempted almost automatically because of the nature of their work, which of course makes the burden greater for the rest. The sorry fact is that most educated and experienced men and many women never serve on juries, while others do substantially more than their share.

Happily, there was a very encouraging response to this series of complaints, to the effect that extensive reforms in both the selection and use of jurors are in process, due to the interest of such people as Chief Justice Burger of the Supreme Court, Justice Paul Reardon of the Massachusetts Supreme Judicial Court, and others. After six years of effort, a system is now being evolved that can predict the use of jurors' time so that the number called can be more accurately determined. Perhaps even better, there is now a bill in the Massachusetts legislature that would establish in Suffolk Court, on an experimental basis, a system for selecting jurors that would exempt no one, not even lawyers, the governor, or a justice of the Supreme Judicial Court. Such people could be challenged of course, but they would not be exempted. Population projections show that once every ten years every citizen in Massachusetts would then be called on to serve as a juror for a period of one day!

Other avoidable delays were pointed out by a discussant who is a public defender. "There is no reason," she said, "for a lawyer to delay a trial by showing up at ten-thirty or eleven o'clock when he is due at ten, or for a defendant to appear at eleven and keep everybody else waiting. Too many lawyers are willing to postpone cases because they've got 'another appointment,' and many judges are not tough enough in bringing cases along for trial and forcing lawyers to prepare their cases on time."

She added, "But on your point about pathology, Professor Freund, one reason it looms so large is that it is the only part of law most people become aware of. John Doe never thinks about the contract he signs when he buys his new Nova until for some reason it hits the courts — maybe the car is stolen or maybe it's repossessed. Then all of a sudden the fine print becomes important. Every survey in the last ten years on what problems bother people places crime very high, though now it may be running a close race with unemployment and the economy. Crime in the streets, the treatment of criminals. And when people come into the courts, it's mainly crime they see. They listen to the kinds of things people are capable of doing to one another, and read the sentence in the paper, or learn that so-and-so has been excused by the trial judge.

"I am not sure that we as lawyers acquit ourselves well in that process, or that it's what we want ourselves to be judged by. Something has to be done to improve the quality of the criminal justice we are dispensing. As far as I am concerned it is delays that are the crux of the problem. I as a prosecutor have serious felony cases that remain untried for much too long, mainly for the reasons Professor Freund just cited: the failure of legislatures and of state governments to find the judiciary, to have enough courthouses, enough courtrooms, enough personnel, to handle them. Also the lack of money to pay prosecutors a decent salary — and public defenders as well — so they won't be forced to accept other business on the side in order to make a living. Moreover, witness fees are so low, and witnesses have to wait so long, that it costs them basic wages to perform their legal duty. The same is true of a plaintiff, who may lose pay for delay in a court in which he is obliged to appear — after being held up at knifepoint!"

It was agreed that having more prosecutors is not the whole answer. Every week in Suffolk Superior Court there are cases ready for trial, but no courtrooms to try them in, and no judges. Better pay for the existing staff would help. A prosecutor who can give full time to his job can turn in a much better performance than one who has to moonlight. Now, the good ones stay three or four years, and then leave.

And most of our prosecutors need better training. The level of representation in the criminal courts is dreadful, and the law schools are just beginning to train people as trial lawyers. Under the British system, which on the whole operates more effectively than ours, the trial lawyers, or "barristers," are generally separate from the general lawyers, or "solicitors," and the English trial lawyers are real pros. Moreover, in England only 3 percent of civil cases are tried by juries, those dealing with libel, slander, and arrest. This makes a tremendous difference in the load. We could learn from the British.

Our courts are choked. In Suffolk County, Massachusetts, there are 5000 defendants waiting to be tried, and there are always fifty or sixty homicides among them. Add to this that at least in Suffolk County on any given day 80 percent of the cases are continued — that is four out of five on an average list of forty to fifty will have at least one more day in court. A judge in session recently said, "Your figures are way off. You say we're six years behind. We're not six years behind. We're nine years behind!"

2

The Economic Foundation of Freedom

LOUIS O. KELSO

A dynamic and persuasive speaker, economist, investment banker, and author Louis O. Kelso, on an afternoon late in October, sketched a bold plan for worker participation in corporate enterprise. Mr. Kelso believes that no modern economy can realize the full potential of its technology toward eliminating poverty and equalizing economic opportunity until large numbers of its working population become part owners of the instruments of production and so can afford to buy and enjoy all that the economy is capable of producing. To make this possible, he has created a technique for financing workers' ownership of stock in the companies they work for, a device that is being used by several hundred corporations under present circumstances, but which, carried to its ultimate effectiveness, would be financed by what he calls "pure credit." His address at New England Life Hall on October 30 explained this scheme and painted a glowing picture of its potential.

Mr. Kelso holds a B.S. degree in finance, cum laude, *and an LL.B. degree from the University of Colorado, where he was editor-in-chief of The Rocky Mountain Law Review and later taught constitutional law and municipal finance. Formerly a corporate, financial, and tax lawyer, Mr. Kelso is president of Kelso & Company, Incorporated, a San Francisco investment banking firm specializing in the application of financial techniques based on*

16

two-factor theory to a wide variety of business problems. He is director of a number of corporations, and of the Institute for Philosophical Research and the Institute for the Study of Economic Systems. He is co-author of three books, The Capitalist Manifesto, The New Capitalists, and Two-Factor Theory: The Economics of Reality.

IT SEEMS to be time, as John D. Rockefeller III has reminded us in the title to a book he published a couple of years ago, for a second American Revolution. The first American Revolution and the year-by-year refinements of the ideas of the Founding Fathers have contributed more than any other event in history to the development of the political mechanism of a free republic, to what we call political democracy.

Yet there is a vast and obvious problem that we have not yet solved. We still lack a sound and just economic foundation for our political democracy. Our economy is not only a source of frighteningly expanding conflicts within our society, it is in fact designed for conflict. The late historian Arnold Toynbee commented that automation had made masses of the labor force redundant, but that those who continue to be necessary have been authorized by law to organize unions whose "solidarity gives them a monopoly, and this monopoly gives them a strangle-hold." Strikes in public service that supply the daily necessities of life can paralyze society instantly. Strikes in industries whose products are not daily necessities can ruin these industries by putting their costly plants out of action. In this situation, the distribution of society's aggregate real income is determined not by the social value of people's work, but by their ability to paralyze society quickly. Thus the present situation puts a premium on the ability to damage society immediately, while it does not reward the ability to benefit society eventually. "The redistribution of society's aggregate income on this basis," said Mr. Toynbee, "augurs ill

17

for society's prospects." Yet this is the basis for redistribution that is being dictated by the new balance of power.

I do not know anyone who has put the problem any better. Charles Beard pointed out that Edmund Burke gave up the search for a sure fix on the internal causes that necessarily affect the fortunes of a state. He had this comment: "In the field of natural science, such a confusion is a plea of intellectual bankruptcy. Indeed, the very research in mechanics and chemistry that produced the machine age has torn asunder the foundations of the old social order, released new and terrifying forces, and now threatens the dissolution of society itself." But because he felt he had some insight into the causes of strife, Beard was unwilling to give up his search for the cause of social disorder. He continued: "Long the victim of natural forces, man has, by taking thought, made himself master of the wind, the wave, and the storm. May he not, by taking thought, lift himself above the social conflicts that destroy civilizations, and make himself master of his social destiny? Perhaps not. But as the human mind is greater than the waterfall, which it compels, or the lightning-flash, which it confines, so the control of human destiny is a nobler object of inquiry than the search for mechanical power. Even though every other door be slammed in our faces, we must continue to knock."

Beard thought, and I am here to urge, that the great bulk of our social ills stems from our failure to have developed a suitable economic foundation upon which to base our political democracy.

Our dominant theories, and the institutions constructed on those theories, lag centuries behind our political concepts and institutions. In particular, I will seek to convince you, our chief social defect lies in our failure to comprehend how goods and services are produced, and our failure to comprehend the functional significance of property or capital in a free society. The Founding Fathers, particularly John Adams, Thomas Jefferson, and later Daniel Webster, had, I believe, some accurate insight into the relationship between the distribution of productive capital and personal freedom, and the smooth running of our social institutions. Adams wrote: "The only possible way, then, of preserving the balance of power on the side of equal liberty and public virtue, is to make the acquisition of land easy to every member of society; to make a division of land into small quantities, so that the multitude may be possessed of landed estates. If the multitude is possessed of the balance of real estate, the multitude will have the balance of power, and in that case the multitude will take care of the liberty, virtue, and interest of the multitude, in all acts of government." Of course in Adams' day, the U.S. economy was agrarian; land was the principal form of capital, and Adams, like Thomas Jefferson, could urge the broad ownership of land as an adequate way of providing the economic foundation for a political republic or a political democracy.

In John Adams' day perhaps 95 percent of the value of productive capital in the economy was in the form of land. Today it's something less than 6 percent. So you can see that the economic problem, as it relates to the ownership of capital, cannot be solved in terms of mere land distribution.

Daniel Webster, the great senator from Massachusetts, issued this warning and prophecy. "The freest government," he said, "if it could exist, would not long be acceptable, if the tendency of the laws were to create a rapid accumulation of property in few hands, and to render the great mass of population dependent and penniless. In such case the popular power must break in upon the rights of property, or else the influence of property must limit and control the exercise of popular power. Universal suffrage, for example, could not long exist in a community where there was inequality of property. The holders of estates would be obliged, in such case, either in some way to restrain the right of suffrage, or else such right of suffrage would ere long divide the property."

Charles Beard summarizes Webster's wisdom on this point.

"The form of government is determined, except where the sword rules" — that is to say, except in a totalitarian order — "by the nature and distribution of property. Republican government, to be stable, must be founded on men's interests. Property, to be secure, must have a direct interest in representation and a check in the government. Disturbances in countries arise principally from conflicts of groups resulting from variations in the form of distribution of property. Universal suffrage is incompatible with great inequality of wealth. Political wisdom requires the establishment of government-owned property and the control of its distribution through the regulation of alienage and transmission."

So much for the wisdom of the Founding Fathers. I think it was Pope Leo XIII who advised that when a society is perishing, it should be recalled to the principles from which it sprang. And I think it is well that we do so today.

Writing several decades after these events, Alexis de Tocqueville in his masterwork, *Democracy in America*, observed that Americans were still firm in their thinking about property. He said, "In no country in the world is the love of property more active and anxious than in the United States. Nowhere does the majority display less inclination for those principles which threaten to alter, in whatever manner, the laws of property." But between 1835, I think it was, when *Democracy in America* was published, and 1930, the American economy had broken down. And changes began to take place that caused the great jurist Roscoe Pound to note, in 1939, "It is significant that the current of thought which is giving up the idea of property is also giving up the idea of liberty."

My interest was drawn to the subject of economics by the enigma of the Great Depression. The production and distribution of goods and services, it seemed to me, was and is today a physical phenomenon. Yet we had an economy in 1930, and I think we have an economy today, with enormous, indeed almost immeasurable physical power to produce more. And yet, we cannot today, as we could not in the late 1930s, put the two together. This power to produce exists side by side with massive poverty, poverty that government has alleviated by closing the gap in purchasing power by deficit financing, which has led to such events as the impending bankruptcy of one of our largest cities. In the 1930s this puzzling set of phenomena, the existence of productive power, the great desire to consume, and the willingness to work, caused me to begin a search into the causes of the apparent human perversity that kept the machinery from turning properly. I reasoned that it was a capitalist society, and that if one merely learned its principles, one could then find out what was creating the difficulty, what was holding up the show. Much to my horror, research led me to the discovery that there was no theory of capitalism! The word "capitalism" was invented by its enemies. The literature on capitalism then, as now, is a literature of vilification on why it should be stamped out, eliminated from society, and replaced by some other form of economy.

Today we stand with our largest railroads in bankruptcy, our largest cities and our major airlines teetering on the brink of it, two of our largest banks having gone bankrupt, millions of unemployed, billions spent on defining goals, and tens of billions spent on boondoggle — the artificial creation of jobs that otherwise wouldn't exist except as a means of distributing income by government. We have had almost fifty years of Keynesian economics, which holds that society can solve the income distribution problem exclusively through full employment.

Yet today, not only is the American economy in trouble, but no economy on earth is working satisfactorily. Inflation, unemployment, inability to utilize physical productive capabilities fully, are common phenomena around the world. This points to the strong possibility — indeed I may say the inevitability — of a common structural defect. I think that I can identify that defect, and, in doing so, answer the practical

questions as to what we can do about it and how we may return to an era of prosperity, such as we enjoyed in the limited
period of about thirty years after the Civil War. In the process, I will return to the wisdom of the Founding Fathers, who
maintained that a broad distribution of the ownership of productive capital is critical to the operation of a free society with
universal suffrage.

When Adam Smith in *The Wealth of Nations* laid down the
concept of the determination of value objectively under the
laws of supply and demand, and the laissez-faire school of
economists arose to urge that the free market was the best of
all possible economic orders, the French mercantile economist
J. B. Say wrote an article in which he enunciated the principle
we have come to know as Say's Law. In a market economy, he
said, for any given time period, the market value of the goods
and services produced is exactly equal to the purchasing
power automatically created by the process of production. The
laissez-faire followers of Adam Smith hailed Say's Law as absolute proof of the soundness of the proposition that the free
market was the perfect economy. Say had proven, they said,
that because everyone wants to live better, all will maximize
their productive efforts, and as they produce more and more
goods and services, the purchasing power they automatically
create is absolutely adequate to take all the goods and services
off the market. There can be no economic cycles. There can
be no underconsumption, no overproduction. It will be the
best of all possible worlds unless government should make the
mistake of getting its hands on the economic order. The req-
uisite is that the government keep its hands off interest rates,
off labor rates, off import restrictions, off export restrictions.
Let the free market function and everything will be beautiful.

Oddly enough, Say's Law has never been refuted — on
paper. But of course, it never worked on the ground. Every
depression became worse than its predecessor. Every surge in
the economic cycle produced higher peaks and deeper valleys

than before. Why? How could there be a principle of economics, presumably a science, a social science, that rhetorically couldn't be refuted, and yet in practice couldn't be used?

Perhaps there is an answer. In all prevailing schools of economic thought, in Smith's day as in ours, there is an assumption, explicit or implicit, that there is but one factor of production — labor. This will undoubtedly shock you, if you haven't thought about it. The economic policy of the United States, representative of the free-market economies of the Western world, is absolutely identical in this respect with the economic policy of the U.S.S.R. In Russia, the Soviet constitution has a provision that says, in so many words, there is but one factor of production — labor! If you don't work, you can't eat. The national economic policy in the United States is more subtly worded but it says exactly the same thing. It is set forth in the Employment Act of 1946, which says, in effect: It is the economic policy of the United States to solve the income distribution problem — the purchasing power gap — solely through full employment. To the extent that that doesn't work, we have to use welfare.

Two-factor economic theory takes issue with this one-factor concept. Incidentally, one-factor thinkers, whether of the socialist or nonsocialist school, are not unaware of the existence of capital instruments; that isn't the point. The point is that they treat land, structures, and machines — capital instruments in general — as if those instruments somehow or other mysteriously amplified the productiveness of labor.

The whole rhetoric of the rising productivity of labor is built on this myth. Two-factor theory takes sharp issue with the myth. It says that if you really want to understand the distributive dynamics of a free market, free society, a private property society, you need only divide the input factors into two sweepingly all-inclusive categories: the human factor, or labor, meaning everyone from the chairman of the board down to the man who sweeps the sidewalk, and the nonhuman factor, or capital instruments, meaning everything external to man that is capable of being owned and capable of being employed in production — generally speaking, land, structures, and machines.

Two-factor theory has an axiom on the significance of technological change with respect to the two factors. It holds that each of the factors produces or contributes to the production of goods and services in precisely the same senses, the same physical sense, the same economic sense, the same political sense, and indeed the same moral sense. In other words, one can just as morally, and just as soundly economically, and just as soundly politically contribute to the production of goods and services and thus provide purchasing power or income for oneself through the employment of one's capital, as through the employment of one's labor. The point obviously is a property point. The reason a slave, for example, doesn't own what he produces is that his master owns his labor power. So the property question in the case of the human factor is identical with the property question in the case of the nonhuman factor. Technological change shifts the burden of production off the human factor onto the nonhuman factor. Thus every single step in this accelerating process is a process that diminishes the adequacy of a man's labor power to enable him to consume his share of what both capital and labor produce. He can only compensate for this loss by acquiring — legitimately — property ownership in the other factor of production: capital.

When you think of Say's Law in terms of *two* factors of production, the validity and usability of the Law become immediately apparent. If there are two factors of production, and if those factors are widely distributed throughout the consumer units of the society, and if the units are all engaged in production, or if each consumer is engaged in production, either through his labor power, his privately owned capital, or some combination of the two, then the consumer is entitled, by reason of the protection of his private property in that factor of production, to income that enables him to support production, support himself, and support his standard of living.

But notice this. The reason for the division of the input factors into two categories *is* a property point. The diffusion of the ownership of labor power is totally atomized within any free society. One man, one labor power. One woman, one labor power. The ownership of the nonhuman factor is not subject to any such rules whatsoever. It can be concentrated ad infinitum. Let me show you what that means.

Say there is a single individual — that his name is John Paul Getty. And say that *Time* magazine is right when it estimates the value of the capital he owns at $4 billion. At the rate of return he probably receives on his invested net worth, I would assume that he has an income that would support twenty-five, or thirty, or thirty-five thousand families — at affluent levels of income.

Now, does production furnish its own demand, when one man has the productive power capable of supporting twenty-five, thirty, thirty-five thousand families? Suppose he can consume as much as ten affluent families, or twenty, or a hundred. He still will have incredible excess income. What does he do with it? He can only channel it back into the acquisition of more productive power. What then? He has greater excess income and greater excess need to acquire greater productive power. Thus the mismatch between the possession of unsatisfied needs and wants, and the possession of the power to produce — not to receive, but to produce — the means of satisfying those needs and wants increases in magnitude.

Say's Law tells us that if you want to cure poverty you raise the productive power of the individuals who are poor. In this country we have spent forty-five years attacking the *effects* of poverty, not the *causes*. If a man can't educate his children, we provide educational subsidies. If he can't pay his doctor bills, we provide health subsidies and hospital subsidies. If he can't buy a home, we give him rent subsidies, or public housing subsidies, and so forth. Every one of these is an attack on the *effects* of poverty. Not a single one is an attack on the *cause* of poverty. And of course, no attacks on the effects of poverty can ever reduce it. The only way we can eliminate, or even reduce, poverty is to attack its cause, *to build greater productive power into the masses.*

I believe that if the value of labor were measured by market forces, that is, by the law of supply and demand, then during the period of recorded history, say from 3000 B.C. to the present, capital and labor, the human and the nonhuman factors of production, would have roughly traded places in their respective production significances. Labor certainly produced, or provided, well over 90 percent of the input at the beginning of history. Today, I'm certain that it provides well under 10 percent of the productive input. You'll quickly recognize that most of the legislative countermeasures that we've taken since 1930 are measures designed to eliminate, or to repeal, the law of supply and demand as it applies to this basic ingredient of input. We have minimum wage laws. We have all sorts of laws requiring the payment of higher and higher wages on public contracts. We even went so far as to give the power to organized labor to use physical coercion to get more and more in return for less and less work. Rule by physical coercion or force is the opposite of rule by law. Yet we were desperate in the 1930s and we had no better answer.

If what I have said up to this point is sound, then, as you reflect on it, you would think that our institutions should be adjusting to this technological change. You would think that as labor power became less and less adequate in the picture, or provided less and less input into the production mix, the world of finance, which is the matrix of new capital formation, would be taking measures to broaden the base of property ownership, the ownership of productive capital, in order to offset the effect of the diminishing input of labor as the result

26

of technological change. Let me explain why these measures have not been taken.

When a corporation believes it can sell an additional number of its goods or services, it does a market or feasibility study. It does a feasibility study because feasibility is the heart of corporate financial logic. The feasibility study not only determines what the cost of growth will be, but it also estimates, by projection and careful analysis, how long it will take that capital to pay for itself. The liquidation of the cost of new capital formation within a reasonable period of time — and a rule of thumb is three to five years — is the heart of the logic of corporate finance.

The corporation, having also done its market study, determines that it will cost a million dollars to expand its plant to fill the market. Under the techniques of conventional corporate finance, the corporation can finance the expansion out of internal cash flow; that is, it can earn profits, pay its taxes, accumulate cash until it has the million dollars, and then buy its new plant or equipment. Or it can go to a lender, bank, or an insurance company, and borrow a million dollars, if it convinces the lender that the feasibility study is sound, and pay off the loan over a period of years. It can also finance through the investment credit, which is simply a law that permits the diversion of money from taxation into capital costs; from accelerated depreciation, which is similar in effect; and from depletion allowances, which apply to the natural resource industries, giving tax allowances to finance growth. These techniques, which, in the aggregate, if averaged over the past fifteen years, account for 98 percent of the new capital formation, have one characteristic in common: When the financing process is completed, *not a single new stockholder has been created.* In other words, 98 percent of the techniques of business finance are designed to expand the power to produce, but to leave the ownership of that power in the hands of a stationary, if not shrinking, ownership base.

Nor does the sale of stock to the public for cash change this situation one iota — because the only people who have the cash are the 5 percent of the consumer units who own all the productive capital. They alone have the excess cash over and above the needs to pay their living costs, their housing installments, their automobile installments, their TV installments, and so forth, to invest in newly issued stock. Thus, whereas in the world of technology, we are changing the relative input significance of the factors of production, in the world of finance, we are bringing into existence in excess of $100 billion worth of newly formed capital every year, and building that ownership into an absolutely stationary base. Indeed, it is actually a shrinking base, because the number of shares issued to individuals in many years is less than the number of shares repurchased by corporations.

This is why we have a society designed for conflict. Functionally speaking, we have an economy designed to build incremental productive power into people having no unsatisfied needs or wants, present or potential. And it is designed to deny that incremental productive power to the masses who make up the customers of the economy, and who are alienated and resentful of being left in a position where they cannot be self-sufficient and self-supporting.

One might say that the modern corporation has embarked on a strategy of annihilating its customer constituents, or at least their power to consume. It eliminates their jobs through automation and their power to become stockholders through conventional finance. Here, clearly, is the error in the structure in our society that the Founding Fathers saw in terms of land ownership. Because the world looked so big to them that it seemed we would never run out of land, and because they failed to foresee the shifting of the productive importance from land to structures and machines, they did not lay down rules that we could follow, through which we could apply their advice, so clearly reasoned at the beginning of the Republic.

28

Can it be changed at this late date? Fortunately, it can, once we make up our minds where the difficulty lies and determine to correct it. The logic of corporate finance is the purchasing of capital on terms where it will *pay for itself.* The legal design of the enterprise, its financial design, and the allocation of credit determine who becomes the owner of the newly formed capital. By designing a series of financing tools and using the basic logic of business, we have shown that it is possible to build ownership literally into anyone, but we think that priorities, when carefully sifted, make a strong case for building ownership first into the labor force. The U.S. economy today is capable of producing a high standard of living for perhaps the top 7, 8, 9 percent of the people — the 5 percent who own all the productive capital and a few highly paid professionals outside that class. It is not capable of producing a high standard of living for the rest. They are all poor in differing degrees. The most awesome poverty is on the bottom, but some of the most frightening poverty is in the middle class, where the husband works, and probably moonlights; where the wife works, and she too may moonlight; where they're up to their eyeballs in debt. While they may look affluent to the world, they indeed are very poor, as is the quality of their lives. Their children are alienated and grow into strife-torn adults.

The employee stock ownership trust — ESOP, as it is popularly known — is the most popular of the financing techniques designed to solve this problem. It is suitable for use in corporations of any size engaged in any line of business.

Capital in a well-managed business will pay for itself. But it will not pay for itself if the state and federal governments take 56 percent or 58 percent, or in New York City 61 percent, of the wealth produced by capital in the form of corporate income taxes, and the board of directors may take up to 100 percent of what is left. The board is under no legal obligation to pay out the wages of capital, as it is the wages of labor. If it does determine to pay out some of those wages of capital in the form of dividends, all the taxing jurisdictions jump on the individual stockholder and, depending on his income bracket, take away varying amounts of his income. Under such conditions it is perfectly obvious that there is no way to buy capital in the marketplace and pay for it out of what it produces. We need the pretax dollar to put the average workingman in this position. To do so, we appropriated the tools of deferred compensation. Back in 1921, Congress passed a law authorizing tax-exempt employee trusts, called stock bonus trusts. Those trusts were the forerunners of the ESOP, or Employee Stock Ownership Plan, trusts.

For an ESOP we establish a trust within a company, and, using the same facts, invite the lender to make his loan not to the corporation directly, but to the trust, which is operated by a committee, normally appointed by the board of directors. The trust then invests the proceeds of the loan in newly issued stock of the corporation. This puts the money back in the corporation, so that it can finance its expansion. The trust gives back its note to the lender. Stock equivalent to the value of the investment is issued to the trust, and the corporation, to make the transaction financible, guarantees to the lender that, as installments of the trust's note fall due, it will make a payment into the trust sufficient to enable the trust to pay off its debt. That amount is diminished, of course, by the dividends paid into the trust.

The tax explanation of this arrangement is that the corporation has set up a qualified employee benefit trust and makes payments into it that are deductible from corporate income taxes. But let me give you the two-factor economic theory explanation of what is happening.

First, the logic of finance, from the standpoint of the traditional stockholder, is that he has access through his corporation to nonrecourse credit. That credit is used to buy incremental productive power that builds additional income-producing power behind his stock. It either provides more income for him or raises its value as viewed from the standpoint of the public market.

The employee stock ownership trust makes this logic available to the worker. The employee, through his trust, has access to a loan — for which he has no personal liability — that is used to buy newly issued stock under terms whereby the corporation commits itself to make a high payout of the wages of capital in pretax dollars, as permitted by law. Thus, the employee can pay for his stock out of what the underlying capital produces. Approximately 140 of these plans have been put into effect in companies ranging from small ones with annual sales of $100,000 to $500,000 a year, to corporations with sales in excess of a billion dollars a year. Such plans function extraordinarily well. So powerful indeed is this technique, and so productive its capital, that in a number of cases employees have bought their companies outright and paid for them in three or four years, *without taking anything out of their pockets or paychecks.*

This technique, if used on a massive scale and supplemented by laws that greatly increase its attractiveness to the corporation, the employee, and the labor union, can turn around the U.S. economy by building market power into the masses.

Let us now add two new institutions. One I call a capital diffusion insurance corporation (CDIC). Such an entity does not exist today, but the precedent for it is well established. It is nothing but a capital financing counterpart of the FHA housing insurance program, an insurance arrangement that insures lenders who make qualified loans for housing. Since the CDIC would insure lenders to business enterprises on loans that would normally pay for themselves out of the expansion of capital, its premium should be a fraction of the ½ percent per year charged by FHA, perhaps ⅛ percent, or 1/16 percent. The second institutional change needed to carry this technique to its logical extreme is to make the ESOP notes of the trust held by lenders discountable at the Federal Reserve

Bank. And the discount rate should not exceed the administrative costs of the Federal Reserve Bank. My estimate is that the figure should not exceed ½ percent.

In this technique of financing, which should be limited to basic, well-managed, self-liquidating new capital formation in established enterprises, the rate of interest should comprise the insurance premium, the discount rate of the Federal Reserve Bank, and a fair return to the lender, who reviews the initial feasibility and services the debt, making certain that the covenants of the loan agreements are observed and that the payments are made. A rate of 1 or 2 percent will provide an excellent profit to the lender — a sum in line with traditional banks' "spreads," or the difference between interest paid to depositors and interest charged borrowers. Under these circumstances, I need not dwell on the significance of a 2, 2½ percent, or 3 percent effective interest rate to borrowers, compared to the prevailing 10, 12, 14 percent from which we are suffering today, in terms of getting the economy back on a growth track.

In an economy that has removed all institutional barriers to economic growth, it should no longer be possible to ask the question, where do we get the money for this railroad, that rapid transit system, or the power plants canceled in the last two years because of lack of sufficient financing. Pure credit uses the power of people to contract with each other under a legal system that enables everyone to enforce or defend his rights under the contract. There is no limit to it except the physical limits of the economy. If we run out of resources domestically, or cannot acquire them through trade, we are up against a physical limit, which is also a business and financing limitation. If we run out of manpower, that is another physical limitation. I think we will be able to achieve twenty-five to thirty years of legitimate full employment in the U.S. economy when we change our economic policy from a one-factor to a two-factor policy, with annual growth rates reaching 12,

14, and 15 percent as Japan did in the past decade. A final physical limitation might be that we will run out of knowhow, but I consider that unthinkable.

Notice that this is a technique for monetizing tools, for monetizing self-liquidating productive capital. Compare this with what we do today, when, under conditions of labor surplus, we raise government salaries and veterans' pensions, or pay labor unions more and more pay for less and less work. Each one of these cases is an instance of *monetizing welfare*. This explains inflation. This is why we have reduced the value of the dollar twice in recent years. As the Organization for Economic Cooperation and Development bankers have said for fifteen years, if you keep on monetizing welfare, you will destroy the dollar. It will no longer be usable in international trade. And of course it becomes less and less adequate in domestic trade.

The two-factor economy, on the other hand, is a deflationary economy. In it most men will gain more and more affluence by the increasing purchasing power of their money. If there is any inflationary impact, it will be brief. I believe there will be none, because the growth of the economy, once we begin to build market power into the masses, will be such as to pull people off welfare and out of government employment because of more attractive opportunities in industry. Nevertheless, even if we assume that there is an inflation, it will be brief, for in two, three, four, or five years the capital will have thrown off enough output to reverse the inflationary forces. From that point forward it is possible for capital to create goods and services indefinitely. Its productive power is preserved by depreciation, which is taken out of gross income before net income is computed. And that depreciation is calculated to be adequate to restore and maintain the productive power of the capital tools.

Thus we can visualize a society expanding at rates never before achieved in the United States. It will build market power into the masses; it will be deflationary; and it will have nothing to do whatsoever with the federal budget. Funds discounted through the Federal Reserve Bank do not become part of government's fiscal operations in any sense of the word.

You may wonder why I have gone into detail and not spoken in generalities. Let me say it is because I agree with William Blake, the English poet, when he said, "He who would do good to another must do it in minute particulars. General good is the plea of the scoundrel, the hypocrite, and the flatterer, for art and science cannot exist but in minutely organized particulars."

What we have been doing is asking the wrong questions. We have asked, how can we enable people to consume more? And we have given answers that will never solve the problem of the cause of poverty. We need to shift our focus to ask, how can we make people more productive? The answer is, only by enabling people to acquire capital ownership. Two-factor theory tells you that once a worker reaches maturity, that is to say, fully knows his job, there is no way to raise his productiveness. To make him more productive as a means of enabling him to achieve a higher legitimate income, without coercion or welfare disguised as wages, it is essential for him to acquire significant ownership of capital.

It is not too late, two hundred years after our political Revolution, to carry out a bloodless, violence-free, constructive, *almost imperceptible* economic revolution that will assure the regeneration, self-renewal, and perpetuation of the free society we celebrate in the Bicentennial. The techniques of corporate finance are easily adaptable. They are advantageous to the corporation and the economy; they eliminate future welfare; they build a future tax base that will dwarf anything heretofore dreamed of; and, I believe, form the missing link to enable this society to guide the rest of the world to similar economic regeneration and self-renewal as it looks to us for leadership.

Questions and Discussion

The discussion of Mr. Kelso's address at the Parkman Center later that evening was one of the liveliest of the entire series. In addition to a banker and several businessmen, the panel included the Treasurer, the Auditor, and the Director of Human Services of the City of Boston, and a professor of economics. There was plenty of informed interest in the ESOP.

The biggest single question in the minds of the panelists concerned "pure credit," the foundation stone on which the largest possible application of the plan rested, the mechanism by which the workers' shares in the ownership of companies would ultimately be financed if conventional sources prove inadequate. Kelso explained that "credit is nothing but the power of the people to contract with each other. All you have to do to use it is to be a member of the human race, a part of the society and the economy. When you use pure credit you're using the one social element in economics. Pure credit involves the use of the Central Bank — in our case the Federal Reserve — as a method of closing a contract between two or maybe many people which is payable in money."

As an example Kelso cited an ESOP loan discounted with the Federal Reserve Bank. Asked for a "non-ESOP example," he said that if the Boston Edison Company were to borrow $50 million from the First National Bank of Boston, and the bank could discount the loan directly with the Federal Reserve Bank, this would be pure credit. The bank would not be lending this money out of its "long, blue stockings," but would be using "the social power of the society," "the power of people to enter into contracts with one another." Japan used pure credit to finance her industrialization before World War II. She had no savings and she borrowed nothing, yet she created a powerful economy.

It was objected that this use of pure credit would in fact be the creation of money by the Federal Reserve, and would have a powerful inflationary effect. Mr. Kelso argued that it would not be inflationary, that it was a process which had no limit, that it was not creating money but "monetizing productive capacity," that is, borrowing against present or future savings in order to increase productive capacity and thus increase profit for both the original 5 percent of stock owners and the 95 percent who would become owners of capital through the ESOP.

Kelso pointed out that when one uses pure credit there is no justification for the high interest rates of the traditional system in which borrowing has been possible only for the few, the 5 percent, the rich. "If we're going to make credit available to the many, the poor," he said, "then we've got to get the rates down to the point where they will become highly productive in a short period and will speed capital formation from the 3 percent or 4 percent where it has been for the past 100 years to 14 percent or 15 percent. To achieve this goal the interest rate for such loans has to be around 2 to 3 percent." There are, in short, two kinds of interest. The kind we're accustomed to, and this other kind which should be limited to the cost of its three elements: the administrative cost to the Central Reserve Bank, the cost of the risk, which may be determined by actuarial principles, and the profit to the private enterprise lender who does the feasibility study, monitors the loan, and makes certain that it is paid off.

Again it was objected that the proposed interest rates, as well as the use of pure credit itself, would be inflationary, because it would increase the money supply. And again Kelso argued that it would not: that pure credit should be limited to loans for self-liquidating well-managed businesses. This phase of the argument appeared to be a draw.

"Is the plan useful," one panelist asked, "if a company does not need money for expansion?"

Kelso replied that there are very few corporations that don't have an insatiable demand for new capital. However even in a corporation owned by one man, or a family, with no heirs interested in the business — or facing heavy inheritance taxes at the death of the key owners, an ESOP can be used to provide a market for their stock. The ESOP will enable the company to continue; and the employees will be strongly motivated to improve operations through their company ownership.

An ESOP can also provide needed new capital as a company issues a number of ESOP shares equal to 5 percent, 10 percent, or 15 percent of its payroll, and it converts money it would otherwise pay in taxes into employee ownership.

Private ownership of capital, it was pointed out, provides one of the great benefits of present-day capitalism, "the ability to fail." Under other forms of government you can't fail — if you lack funds you just go back and ask for more. But with us failure is possible, and helps to keep the economic system healthy.

Another panelist suggested that while the ESOP appeared to be useful to the well-established and well-managed business, it would not be adaptable to the small new business trying to get started. Kelso did not wholly agree; he replied that an ESOP could indeed be adapted to a start-up enterprise and has been so used. "We've enabled the employees of Watts Manufacturing to buy it for $5 million. It was financed by Chase Manhattan Bank, and the employees own it 100 percent. But you're right in the main," Kelso went on. "ESOP's most important use will be to connect the noncapital owning worker with the big companies. If we begin to use pure credit to finance the growth of the big basic industries — public utilities, big manufacturing companies, big service industries — the main successful enterprises that have survived five or ten years of performance, then we shall begin to free up accumulated savings for the more speculative things, which have potential for bigger loss and bigger gain.

"Just to give you some idea, the Economics Department at General Electric has estimated that it will take $4.5 trillion to finance the normal economic growth of the next decade. That's four times the rate of capital formation of the last decade. My guess is that they are 50 percent too low. We're talking about the difference between digging an oil well in your back yard and digging halfway up the English Channel. The capital requirements are immensely different. Or you're talking about getting copper from a nice comfortable mine in Arizona and getting it beyond the Arctic Circle. I think just these two examples will show how advantageous it will be if we can learn to use pure credit through ESOPs for the big businesses. If that can be done, then it is possible to do many more things for the small business."

Robert Schneider then asked, "Would you use this seed money in acquisitions?"

Kelso: Yes.

Schneider: Would the risk factor increase substantially?

Kelso: The quality of management determines the quality of the acquisition.

Schneider: Yes, but I think there's a very definite differentiation in risk between acquisition and new product development.

Kelso: Oh, in general I agree. I would say that the acquisition movement, the whole conglomerate movement in the United States was powered by two things: the fact that we have abrogated the laws of private property as they apply to the corporate stockholder, and secondly that although the delegation of the right or the attempt at delegation is legally impossible, nevertheless we have attempted to delegate to labor unions the power to use raw physical coercion to take out more and more while putting in less and less. Increases resulting from the price spiral are thus actually welfare payments, not wages, since they pay for nothing.

Moreover, the stockholder should get his full share of the wages of capital. Before the case of Ford *vs.* Dodge and Cousins, the stockholder was entitled to his dividend, his proportion of the net earnings of the corporation, exclusive of operating reserves. That is, new capital formation was not financed out of earnings. At the time that decision was made, there was no alternative way of financing corporate growth. But while the decision helped with this problem, every state passed laws to the effect that the stockholder has no right to a dividend until it is declared, and management is under no obligation to declare one. Once we provide an unlimited way of financing corporate growth through ESOP, it will be possible to reinstate the law of private property as it applies to the stockholder. This is terribly important if more and more of our population is to depend on capital ownership and not on their labor power ownership.

At this point it was objected that Kelso was "talking a revolution that's a lot broader than just ESOP. You're talking about a rejuvenation of regulatory philosophy and application; you're talking about rejuvenation of a horde of stockholders' rights, and probably a whole new attitude on the part of organized labor."

To this Kelso responded that he was merely trying to make sense out of the economy, and another speaker picked up the theme of labor: "Why in the world would organized labor ever approve of an employee stock ownership plan — if they understood it?" To which Kelso answered that it would give them more power, and two sources of income for labor leaders — a checkoff on wages, and another on capital billed to the employees. Their constituents would become affluent and retire rich. The leaders themselves then wouldn't have to steal in order to become rich — they could do it honestly. And they wouldn't have to live on conflict: they could live on education, communication, constructive help in expanding the system. They don't have to be the Mafia of the U.S. economy. At this point one panelist recalled a cartoon of a laborer picketing a factory and saying, "I feel like a fool. I own a hundred shares of this company."

39

Asked whether ESOPs were ever used in lieu of pension funds, Kelso answered that no, they were generally instituted in companies that already had a pension fund, but that after a few years management came to feel that the fixed benefits of the fund were far less desirable than continued opportunity for growth by channeling the pension money into additional ESOP funding. Likewise, Kelso felt that insurance companies, a prime source of funds, would soon be willing to lend money at the modest ESOP rate of 3 percent, or else the whole country "blows up and follows, as Toynbee says, the nineteen preceding civilizations." He also felt that any loss of federal tax revenue would be more than compensated for by a reduction in welfare spending and in "boondoggle" — that is, money "spent to create phony jobs to legitimate incomes that would never exist if they depended on consumers spending their own dollars to buy goods and services. Add those two things together, and you're talking about 80 to 85 percent of the federal budget.

"The object of this game," he continued, "is to build self-sufficiency into the masses. To enable them to be economically productive, to live well, and to be good consumers. Mass production really needs mass consumption, and not on credit, but by guys who can pay for it.

"When you begin systematically building market power into the masses, you are going to call up an enormous expansion of the productive system. I estimate that our economy must expand from seven to twelve times its present size. That is the most gigantic construction job in the history of man."

Asked what bounds would be set on expansion by ultimate limits to growth, Kelso responded that he didn't subscribe to the limit of growth idea at all. What he anticipated was that increased productive power would "build up a simply titanic tax base," which would practically eliminate the need for welfare, and handily pay whatever welfare burdens there are. "I think we'll suck people off the welfare rolls. I think we'll suck them off public employment. We may even have to open up immigration again in order to satisfy our requirements."

But another panelist returned to the idea of limits. "We do live in a closed system. Earth as a planet has measurable amounts of everything. What do you think are the limits of growth?"

To which Kelso replied, "I think the population must be limited because no matter how affluent people are — even if everybody's a millionaire — if we're thirty-five feet deep in protoplasm it's going to be miserably uncomfortable. But I think the productive capability of the planet is probably a thousand times what we're producing today. Maybe ten thousand times!"

"What about the ecological limitations?"

"Purely a capital problem, not a technical one. It costs a lot of money to produce refined oil from high-sulfur crude and not pump a lot of sulfur and other things into the atmosphere. But we know how to do it; it's simply a matter of money. You solve that problem by raising the productive power of the consumer so he can afford the product or service at its increased cost."

"But ultimately we will run out of resources because we are a closed system. At what point do you think that would happen?"

"I think a lot of that is illusory. If we hadn't got into a kid game of trying to land a spaceship on the moon, and had devoted our time to converting coal into usable energy — let's not forget that the last year of the war the Germans fought with their air force on gasoline made from brown coal, which has about half the energy content of the poorest coal in the United States. If we had faced these problems we would have solved them long ago. We've got the resources, we've got the intelligence. All we need is some brains at the top. That's the missing link."

There was no sign among the panelists of general agreement

with this point of view. It was hard for most to escape the thought that oil shale and Athabasca tar sands to the contrary, our planet is finite and there are limits — even though this view did not have the last word in the discussion.

In the minds of some panelists there appeared to remain a lurking suspicion that pure credit was a shoal concealing real dangers — dilution of stock values, inflation through the creation of vast quantities of new money, and nameless uncertain things perhaps the more frightening because they were not clear.

In conclusion, however, a panelist pointed out that one point which had come out of the discussion is that for two or three generations we've had a face-off between capital and labor, and that whether or not people agreed with Kelso's theory in detail, it is increasingly clear that capital and labor must now become allies, and that the line of separation in the class warfare is not between capital and labor, but between the producers and the nonproducers. Labor must one day wake up to realize that it is on the side of capital, not of welfare.

To this Kelso replied, "I strongly believe my plan represents the cutting edge of change in our society. Either we solve our fundamental economic problem or our society is going to disappear. The economic ideas that have been in the ascendancy for the past forty years have brought us from a disastrous depression to another disastrous depression plus disastrous inflation. I don't think that's progress, and I think I have put my finger on the place where change must occur. I hope those in the relevant disciplines will have the ingenuity — as I am confident they have — to work out the right accommodation with change. Historically it has happened many times. The French College of Surgeons said that Pasteur was wrong, that he was nothing but a chemist. But eventually they came round, and began to wash their hands."

3

Smoke Signals: An Analysis of American Communications by an Ancient Briton

SIR HUW WHELDON

Large and well set up, a handsome man with the air of an actor, the director of the British Broadcasting Corporation Television Service addressed the Bicentennial Forums at Faneuil Hall November 25, 1975. Speaking with great energy in an idiom of his own, he was such a master of amiability and wit that our heads were off before we knew the sword was out. And we laughed in the process. In the gentlest way in the world he told us what he finds wrong with American television, and also a great deal that he finds right with it. He was the sort of speaker one could have listened to all day.

After joining the BBC in 1952, Sir Huw became managing director of BBC–TV in 1969. He is largely responsible for such memorable programs as "Civilization," "America," "The Ascent of Man," "The Six Wives of Henry VIII," "The Forsyte Saga," and "War and Peace." He also serves as chairman of the Court of Governors, London School of Economics. A frequent lecturer, he has made several appearances in the United States on network television, including interviews on David Susskind's "Open End" and "Bill Moyers' Journal."

Before joining the BBC, Sir Huw served the Arts Council of

Great Britain as its Director for Wales and Director of Festivals.
He is a native of Prestatyn, Wales.

I READ an article, some years ago, in a magazine, written by a
film critic. In the first two paragraphs, the critic put a question that seemed to me a good one. The question followed a
statement, and the statement was this: He said he had been a
film critic for thirty years. When he was a boy, nothing had
pleased him more than to go to the movies, and even as a
man, few things pleased him as much as going to the movies.
If there was another thing he liked doing, it was writing. To
be paid both to go to the movies and then to write about those
movies struck him as a virtually ideal existence. And this he
had been doing now for over twenty years.

One question, however, occurred to him from time to time.
And the question was this: That today, by virtue of the speed
of communications across the world, when he went to see a
new movie, more often than not he would already have read
about it in some paper, journal, or magazine, because it would
already have been seen in California, or Britain, or Germany,
or Italy, or somewhere; so that he would already have some
kind of idea of what the movie was like. He did not mind
that. He also was aware that from reading judgments made
on this movie by his peers, people whose judgments he ad-
mired, he would be going quite frequently to a movie that he
would almost certainly enjoy.

Why then, he said — and this was the question — why
then did he have a twinge of disappointment, always and invariably, as he passed the box office because he was not going
to see a new movie with Fred Astaire and Ginger Rogers?
Now that is a good question. It is a question that I have often
asked myself. As I go to see this new movie, I have a definite
twinge of disappointment that it isn't a new movie with
Humphrey Bogart and Lauren Bacall! The reason I have that

44

feeling of disappointment is, of course, that movies with Ginger Rogers and Fred Astaire; movies with Humphrey Bogart and Lauren Bacall; movies with Greta Garbo, Wallace Beery, and James Stewart; and movies called *Mr. Deeds Goes to Town, The Maltese Falcon, The Thin Man,* and *Stagecoach* were above all *very good movies.*

The question arises, what kind of "goodness" did they represent, because clearly we need not be too understanding and eggheaded about it. They were *not* the art of the sublime. *Mr. Deeds Goes to Town* is a lovely movie, but it is not a cathedral. *The Thin Man* provides a great deal of enjoyment, but it is not the Parthenon. Movies, that is to say, coming from Hollywood were not made in the name of an overwhelming idea like Windsor Castle or Chartres. Nor were they made by the driving individual genius of overwhelming talent like George Eliot, or Herman Melville, or John Keats, or Homer, or Sophocles, or Ibsen. If they were not made in the name of an overwhelming idea or in the name of an overwhelming individual, in the name of what was it that they were made? I suggest to you that they were made in the name of something that has become a little déclassé, that has had recently a poorish press but something that is not disreputable. They were made in the name of pleasure. They were calculated to give pleasure, and pleasure they gave. *Mr. Deeds Goes to Town* pleased people, and so did *The Maltese Falcon.* And they were *meant* to please people.

Let me put for a moment the concept of "pleasure" into another kind of perspective. There are many forms of human activity which have deserved well of the world, which have been made in terms of the concept of "pleasure." I will name two for you: cooking and gardens. As against other benighted nations, including, alas, the English and, in my opinion, the Americans as well, the French and the Chinese understood how to invent *menus.* They both invented a method of cooking that has pleased millions of people across the world and

45

across the centuries, and it is not a dismissable thing to have done. I would not like to say that the English, still less the British, invented gardens, but they had a lot to do with cultivating gardens, as they had a lot to do with cultivating sports. Many nations of the world have had much to do with cultivating the notions of spectacle and procession and ceremony. There is a very real sense in which spectacle, ceremony, sport, gardening, and cooking, like movies, have all been made in the name of pleasure. And at their best, successfully made. They are not disreputable inventions.

Television in America and in our country shares in some degree in that process of enjoyment. Yet, in many ways, it is a more complicated process. I myself do not believe — and it is important that I should make this plain — that television in this country is the wilderness of monkeys that it is frequently said to be, not least by Americans. That is to say, an awful lot of television is very popular, and the reason why it is very popular is that it is very enjoyable. And although enjoyment is a little déclassé, it does remain actually enjoyable!

The kind of television I have seen in this country and which I have enjoyed even includes Johnny Carson. I well know that this is a disreputable thing to say. But I enjoy looking at "The Johnny Carson Show," like nearly everybody else. I enjoy "The Mary Tyler Moore Show." Who doesn't? I very much enjoy baseball, although, of course, I am aware that despite my immense admiration for the American people (which is true and clear and understood), it has always seemed to me a perversion that they do not understand soccer! Nevertheless, I do understand, in some degree, that somehow or other they have committed themselves to baseball. And baseball on television is enjoyable, as golf is enjoyable. And Senate hearings are not simply enjoyable, they are riveting! These are programs to be seen on this great continent by millions of people; and it is not up to us, and by us I do not mean me, to do anything other than to realize that the reason why they are enjoyable is that they are meant to be enjoyable. They succeed in that and they are enjoyed!

Yet, they are marred to some degree in British eyes. The first thing that mars them is that there are too many ads. If you are born and bred in our country, it is really very tiresome to sit down and by the time you have had about eight minutes of development you have advertisements. However, I am prejudiced. I was brought up in a different tradition; and there it is.

There is another thing, however. To British eyes, one of the most extraordinary things in American television, which, as I say, is largely enjoyable, and when enjoyable is very much so, is the prevailing absence of the writer. It would seem to me unthinkable as managing director of BBC Television or as a producer in BBC Television, or for that matter as a producer or a director in commercial television in our country, that a year should pass in which you have not at least tried to get plays from the leading playwrights and novelists of the country. If the novelists of the country include Angus Wilson and Kingsley Amis, and the playwrights include Harold Pinter and David Mercer, it would seem unthinkable not to have approached them during the year to say, "Will you please write, not a play, but another play for the BBC?" Pinter would not have been Pinter and Mercer would not have started had there been no BBC.

Now there was a time when there were frequently plays on American television. There were great plays by Paddy Chayefsky, and so on. But today few plays are made and few plays are transmitted; and an Englishman, possibly wrongly, misses the sense of dramatic achievement. This fact is obscured, of course, in this state by the work of WGBH here in Boston, because they, I am delighted to say, import our plays and put them on. And who am I to do anything except be pleased and delighted that this has happened?

I would like at this moment to pay a tribute, if I may, to

WGBH, because in fact it was they who started the process of putting together plays and productions under the title "Masterpiece Theater" (virtually all of which were made by us) which have spread all over the country. It is also they who have taken our productions of the classics, *She Stoops to Conquer*, Shakespearean plays, *The Three Sisters*, Ibsen, Sean O'Casey, and so on, put these together, great classic statements of the human spirit that we have committed ourselves to over the years, and transmitted them as "Classic Theater." I saw one myself last week in San Francisco. To this Boston television arrangement we own a debt of gratitude — we the BBC, we the United Kingdom, and those in this country who enjoy them.

It isn't simply that we are delighted that they have imported work we have done, it is also that we have learned from them. We now do access programs, programs in which the public can speak freely, and we have developed those projects directly in terms of the access programs invented and developed in this great city. And I am glad to acknowledge the fact that that kind of work has taken place. WGBH is exceptional, and there are very few such organizations.

On the whole it is very marked that not many plays are written in this country. Does it matter? Of course it matters. The country is full of writers. The country is full of first-rate minds who are capable of writing books, writing for theaters, and writing for films, and they should be writing for television as well. It is odd that I should say this, because it suits me as a BBC man that they should not. Yet, having been invited to come here, I feel in honor bound to say that this does seem to be the situation.

Plays are, of course, a formality, and we are very formal in England. Here, the process of informality much helps the television programs I have mentioned. In this country, if you are going to take part in a television program, you go to a studio, and when it is time for you to speak, a man waves his finger and it means that it is time to start. It is in point of fact what we do in our country as well. It is called cuing and it is very simple.

When we were restarting television after the war, in 1946 or whenever it was, a group of our production engineers felt that this was altogether too casual a method of doing something so important as to start a program going. So they invented a machine, or engine, which when attached to the person of somebody emitted a vibration at the correct moment and thus warned them that the time had come at last to start speaking.

In those days, we had an announcer called Jasmine Bligh, a very nice and pretty woman. She now lives, I believe, in the United States. Jasmine Bligh was due to start, simply by announcing it, an evening of special programs in May 1946. This engine, or machine, or device, had been invented and it fell to the lot of a friend of mine called Jimmy Redmond, now the chief engineer of the whole BBC, in those days a young, a struggling, boy, to have the honor of strapping this little contraption to Jasmine Bligh's ankle. She was naturally wearing a long dress, because that was the nature of things in England at that time, although it was only half-past four in the after- noon. Jimmy Redmond, trembling, partly because he was so junior, partly because he was lifting a skirt, placed this gadget on Jasmine Bligh's leg. From the engine a cord wound its way across the studio floor and up to the control gallery. As the minutes ticked by, the director asked if everything was ready. They said, yes, that everything was. Half-past four came up, he pressed the button, the gadget vibrated, and Miss Bligh most understandably emitted a short, stifled scream, followed by the words "Good afternoon." The processes of enjoyability are sometimes difficult in England because we are a bit on the formal side. Plays are formal matters, but because of what WGBH has done, those plays are enjoyed here as well.

In *The Oxford Companion to American History*, the first mention of the name Lowell is of a Lowell who was born in 1775, who during the course of his life came across to our country, England, and who then came back here with plans for power looms. It says in *The Oxford Companion to American History*, which I daresay is biased, that this was an illegal and political adventure in which he had taken part. It is a matter of enormous pleasure to me that now this Boston operation, with Lowells still on the Board, is coming across to our country and openly bringing back programs from the BBC.

It is a tradition I naturally applaud, but what has been brought back is largely classical or full-length contemporary drama, and the point I want to impress upon you is that, when I personally talk about the absence of writers, I am not simply talking about the absence of writers in plays. The programs now on American television called "Sanford & Son" and "All in the Family" are based on two important BBC series, one called "Steptoe & Son" and one called "Till Death Us Do Part." The formats were sold. I am very pleased about that too. It all redounds to our glory, and I am delighted.

It is interesting, however, to note that by today the number of episodes of "Sanford & Son" that have been run in this country are well over 200, and the number of episodes of "All in the Family" is moving up toward 200, because they have been running here for nearly four years. They are put on week in and week out, and as we all know, they do very well.

Now, "Steptoe & Son," which is the source of "Sanford & Son," and you'll be surprised to hear this, I think, has had fifty-four episodes transmitted in twelve years. The reason why there have been only fifty-four episodes, which means that on the whole you have only four or five in a whole year, sometimes six, occasionally seven, is because they have been written by writers and that is all writers have had it in them to write. Equally, there have been fewer than forty episodes of "Till Death Us Do Part," the source of "All in the Family," in eight years. Again the reason is the same. They were written by a writer, Johnny Speight, and this is what he had in him to write.

The reason why Ernest Hemingway did not write 40 novels, although his publishers wanted him to; the reason why Raymond Chandler did not write 100 novels, although his publishers would have been delighted (they would have made a lot of money); and the reason why John Updike has not written 70 big books is because they haven't had it in them. Who has? Ten novels is a lot of novels for a novelist, at any time. Ten plays is a lot of plays for a playwright. How many plays did Ibsen write? If, in fact, you are going to insist on having 200 shows and not 50, you can only have them at the cost of making those shows a Raymond Chandler–*type* show. They are not written by Raymond Chandler. They are a Raymond Chandler–type show. That is how we see it. The process of recognizing the work of the writer in England is very important to the nature of the television we make.

Now let us be perfectly clear: a great deal of the television we make is poor because writers, like everybody else, sometimes work badly. A great number of the series fail, and by failure I mean they do not get ratings, or do not gain the admiration of those whose judgment and respect you and I would admire, or both. If they are neither popular nor gain the respect of people whose judgment and admiration you and I would admire, then they have certainly failed; and there are plenty of them. Yet, were it not for those failures, you would not from time to time have works written in terms of a great literary and dramatic tradition. We are very lucky in this, and I do not know why this literary and dramatic tradition has prevailed as it has.

In England actors are two a penny. This is a mystery, but the fact is that there is never any difficulty getting hold of extremely good actors and extremely good actresses. Partly, of course, it is because there are a lot of theaters; partly, of course, it is because there is an imcomparable dramatic tradition.

The fact remains that English actors and actresses are first-rate (I speak as a Welshman by the way). If you want to cast a play in England, as soon as people called Levy and Bernstein turn up, send them home. If their name is Jones or Griffiths, have nothing to do with them. People named O'Sullivan: send them packing at once. People called MacDonald: have nothing to do with them. But if they have names like fresh-water English fish, if they're called Carp or Pike, or Bream or Tench, or Bleak, take them on instantly! Plays featuring Julian Bleak and Dorothy Tench cannot fail! This is simply a rule. Nobody knows why it is. One can only put it down to an overcompensation for many years of "stiff upperlippery" in other forms of social endeavor. Whatever the reason, there are plenty of actors or actresses who will, as it were, enter into the dramatic and literary tradition that presses upon the BBC.

The BBC is a very curious invention, almost a constitutional invention, in the name of which it is possible to lean on this tradition and use it. It is because the constitution by which I work not only enables me, but encourages me, to get at Harold Pinter, and to attempt the classics. And the literary and dramatic traditions of England are so powerful that one way or another it forces itself upon the process of broadcasting.

Now this is difficult in this country. Rightly or wrongly, you set yourselves in a different mold, so that broadcasting is paid for largely by advertising and this has developed a situation of a different kind. Let me make two observations of things that appear curious to me, about what I have seen in England and in this country.

The first is this: This is a country that "gets a move on" and one of the things you have to have in order to get a move on is a suspicion of committees. It is extremely unlikely that great department stores, great universities, or great bridges can be built by committees. By and large, committees are things to

avoid if you want to get a move on. Few people would dis-
agree with this. It has always seemed to me very odd that the
process of writing (whether plays, series, comedies, or documentaries) in this country should be by committee. I have
been from time to time asked how it is that the BBC can fix up
programs like and including the Kenneth Clark series on "Civilization" or the Alistair Cooke series on "America" or the
Bronowski series "Ascent of Man." We have now a man
named Ronnie Eyre looking into religion, which I think will
be a profoundly interesting program series and which is taking three years to make. We have a man from Boston, I need
hardly say, called John Kenneth Galbraith, doing a program on
"Economic Man."

The question is, how does the BBC make these programs? I
will tell you how to do them. It is extremely simple. There is
no difficulty. What you do is this: You find enough money to
start with. That goes for any program. You have got to have
the money. You then find somebody you trust because he is
authoritative, like Kenneth Clark on art, or Alistair Cooke on
the U.S., or, in the matter of economics, someone like John
Kenneth Galbraith. (Economics as material for a program
series is a problem, you know. Everybody talks about economics, but economists themselves, as we all know, are, on the
whole, dull dogs.) Once you have raised the money, you have
got to find authority, in this case an economist you trust, no
matter how difficult. What you have to trust him to be is interesting, illuminating, and stimulating. Then you have got to
find somebody who can work with him and direct the cameras. That is literally all you have to do. You put the one with
the other, fix the budget, and you say, "Come back in three
years' time with thirteen programs."

That is what you do, which actually is what a publisher does
to a novelist. It is what the president of a university does to a
professor. If you are appointed a professor, it is up to you to
sort out a course, do the work, and get on with it. If it's no

good, well, then, you will be fired three years hence. But there is no other way of doing it. It is very, very difficult to teach even law by committee. It is absolutely impossible to write by committee. It is not in the tradition of literature.

So the process of making programs that have some kind of meaning must rely willy-nilly on getting hold of a writer, or a scholar, or a novelist, or a playwright, and trusting him and taking the consequences. Sometimes the consequences are hurtful because the work is boring or bad or miserable, or because your original judgment was poor. But once you have taken him on, you have no alternative, you have to let him get on with it. There is no other way of doing it. If you hire somebody to teach French, it is no use taking her aside all the time, and saying, "Look, start afresh." There is only one way of teaching French and that is to get on with it, as best you can, for better or for worse. We are enabled to do this in our broadcasting arrangements, and it is in its way an overwhelming tribute to our country that this is possible.

Having said that, I am also quite clear that I am saying something which, although true of United Kingdom television, nevertheless leaves unspoken big things about U.S. television. After all, there are good shows — quite apart from programs that are not written (sports, events, Senate hearings, all those marvelous shows) and quite apart from the comic tradition.

We buy a show called "Kojak." We used to buy in the old days a program called "The Dick Van Dyke Show." Another show we bought was "The Man From U.N.C.L.E." These are good shows, and why they are good shows is mysterious to me, because they're written by groups of people, largely, and that tradition is not the tradition of literary creation or of dramatic creation. It is the tradition of advertisement writing. Yet, one way or another, creativity being what it is, somehow or other through all these floorboards, committees, sponsors, and difficulties, "Kojak" comes out, and there's only one word for it — good. I am not suggesting that there are no good shows, but I am suggesting that, on the whole, they seem to come up *in spite of* the system. That is the first observation I have to make.

The second observation I have to make is also a curious one from the point of view of an Englishman. Everybody knows that we are class-ridden. "Upstairs, Downstairs" is the rule in England, as everybody knows. Nevertheless, there is a sort of distinction which we refuse to draw. It is this: there is nobody in this room who does not belong to both minorities and majorities simultaneously. If you are going to talk about majority television on the one hand, and minority television on the other, if there is going to be talk about the thinking man's television on the one hand and television for ordinary people on the other, let me remind you that we are all members of both. I like string quartets. But I also like baseball. I am not pretending; I actually do like both. There are plenty of people who are very keen indeed on news, but they also like "The Mary Tyler Moore Show." Why shouldn't they? The fact is that the process of reaching people in terms both of minority interests and of majority interests is what should take hold of a great mass-communication system.

This is put into silhouette, when you think as a Britisher, of American magazines, which are marvelous, and American publishing, which is magnificent. England has nothing to touch the spectrum you get out of American magazines. By the time you have been here for some weeks, it is clear to you that radio and television are deeply enjoyable; and quite apart from being enjoyable, you also will get great classic statements occasionally imported. All told, it is quite nice, but somehow it does not speak as well for the country as do the magazines. The magazines, and the books above all, speak for the continent. They speak for the Republic. When you look at the magazines (as against our magazines and as against your television) and you go all the way from *Commentary* or *The Atlan-*

tic Monthly by way of *Harper's, Time, Newsweek,* and *Sports Il-lustrated,* right across to *Playboy* on the other end, these magazines are filled with the work of creative people, scholars in their own right, playwrights and novelists in their own right, writing thoughtfully and not simply being celebrities being interviewed.

What you want is for Saul Bellow to write television: to write plays or documentaries as Kingsley Amis and Jacob Bron-owski have done for the BBC. Bellow writes for magazines. *Everybody* writes for magazines. The article is a great Ameri-can invention. Your magazines are packed with the pulse of American thought, using speculative, thoughtful, sometimes delightful, worried, anxious words; speaking of the news, speaking of the future. There's a spectrum of life there that pleases you. If that is true of magazines, so even more is it true of publishing.

It is not up to me to talk about the press and other forms of mass communication. There is one thing, however, I do want to say. The press in this country (as in ours) is under all sorts of attack and getting all sorts of praise. The attacks come from those who say that in recent years the whole notion of objec-tivity, of true and accurate reporting, is being eroded, and that on the whole, the press is moving toward a leftward distortion or a leftist bias. And you hear it said here as in London, in New York as in Liverpool, in Boston as in Manchester. Nor is it necessarily not so. The press does borrow from the climate of cultural opinion, and certainly in my lifetime and certainly in the lifetime of most people in this room, there has been a feeling that the press on the whole was, if anything, rightish. Now there is a feeling that the press is, if anything, leftish. That may be true. I make no such observation. I only make the observation that that may be so. What I do say, how-ever, and it is of immense importance, is that if you come to this country from the outside, one thing is certain, and that is that the press does not tell lies. If you look at television and news, you can ask yourself, "Is this the best way to do the news? Is this news better then the British news? Is British news as good as this news?" There are very difficult technical problems. Today, you are up to the chin in news by half-past four in the afternoon. You could keep news bulletins going for five hours because the communications of the world are so marvelous. Nothing can happen in Delhi, Peking, or anywhere else without us knowing within a matter of moments. If there is an earthquake in Japan or a government falls in Australia, we know at once. A few minutes later, there is film. So that we are drowned in news; there is too much of it; and the question is to select, how to handle it? It is not easy. And so I anxiously watch the handling of news in this country, just as people in this country anxiously watch the handling of news in the United Kingdom. Neither of us is much the wiser. We are all bothered. We do not know how to do it, because there is a very big problem. There is an awful lot of news. In the name of what do you choose what you are going to say? It is not easy.

Yet, having said all that and knowing that it is not easy, you do not feel the presence of liars. There are countries where you do. Here you do not feel when you are reading a newspaper that either the editor or the reporters are in a conspiracy, so handling a thing as to tell you lies. Nobody can do better than be as accurate as he can in his own terms. Accuracy is a very difficult thing to handle. Impartiality is a difficult discipline. Objectivity means having respect for the object. It was Lionel Trilling who reminded us that this was so: it was Matthew Arnold's definition. Objectivity means having respect for the object, so that the object is allowed fair play. It is a difficult thing for reporters to do, at any time. So there are failures, in our country as in yours. But the failure does not feel like lies. It feels more like failure. There is not all that

57

much failure. On the whole, if I watch news on television in this country, I believe it. I do not believe it because Walter Cronkite is venerable. I believe it because I believe it.

I will spend no more time on the news other than to suggest a kind of conclusion. It is this: there are smoke signals going up from this country. The Republic is so great and so powerful that the signals are seen all over the world. And they are confused. I am well aware, of course, as we all are, that, where communications are concerned, it takes two to tell a story — he who tells it and he who hears it. I am well aware that meaning, like beauty, lies in the eye of the beholder and in the ear of the listener. We are all aware of that. I am well aware that anybody is wise to take note of the constant and marvelous injunction "He that hath ears to hear, let him hear." So all communication is difficult. I am aware of that. Who isn't? I am also aware that we all live in a muddled and distracted world, and there are few simple truths to be spoken all over the place.

Having said that, I am aware, in the end, of four powerful thoughts about the smoke signals that come from this country. I could wish that some of the communications were based on different traditions. I could wish that there were improvements here and there, but having said that, I am aware of four traditions. The first is the tradition of *enjoyment*, which I mentioned, and it is not dismissable. It includes not only movies, it includes Tin Pan Alley as a matter of fact. It certainly includes Irving Berlin, Gershwin, Cole Porter, and Rodgers and Hart. It includes an awful lot of television. It includes Hollywood. And it is the note or tradition of enjoyment.

I am aware, secondly, of the note of *truth* that I hear in magazines and in books, although I miss the truthfulness of scholars and writers and poets in much broadcasting.

I am aware in all communication in this country of the note of *freedom;* because even when the things are lousy, which they often are, they feel like bad work by free people. And freedom does not grow on trees either.

Finally, and this may perhaps surprise you a little, to somebody coming to this country from mine (and perhaps this particular occasion is a proper one on which to remember this), there is a possibility of *change* in this great country that is one of the hopes of the world. Boston itself has not been without revolutionary tendencies. Boston itself has not been without the process of exemplifying that change is possible. I am extremely proud of the United Kingdom. I like living there and I am glad I was born there; but it is very difficult to get anything changed. When you come to this country you feel the possibility of change in the air. There are checks and there are balances, and, in practice, I am told on all hands that actually change is much more difficult than I would think. I acknowledge it. I feel its presence in the air, nevertheless. It is very impressive to somebody brought up in Richmond or Islington. That possibility, as I say, is particularly apt here in Boston. I arrived onto an airfield here today, and no sooner was I on this spotless and gleaming airport than somebody told me that it's going to be pulled down in order that some other terminal should be built up because things ought to be changed. And no sooner do I come to this ancient, venerable, and marvelous hall than I am aware that it is in the middle of an area of the city that is changing almost by the hour.

And so, speaking from a conservative tradition, and from a television experience, I salute a Republic in which truth, freedom, and enjoyment are allied to another interesting feature, which is that you can change if you want to, sometimes for the worse, but of course, conceivably, for the better.

Questions and Discussion

The discussion of Sir Huw's address after the Parkman House dinner the same evening was not contentious: there was nothing to argue about. Rather, it brought forth in the form of lucid and informative answers to factual questions what was essentially a second address, on the BBC and how it operates, often in comparison or contrast to American television. These answers covered everything from the organization of the BBC to its handling of violence and sex. We begin with the former.

"Britain has three basic television networks, BBC 1, BBC 2, and ITV or 'Independent Television,' which is made up of a company in Birmingham, one in Manchester, two others in London, and one in Yorkshire. These are all national networks. We in the BBC buy about 14 percent of our programs from America, or wherever. The rest we make ourselves. In addition, in Scotland they want every now and then to do their own programs. They don't want to suffer through those programs made in London. So they make programs called 'The Highlands' or they make Scots plays, or programs about the herring fleets. Now they make about eight hours a week of such programs, and put them out in Scotland; we don't see them in England. Similarly, there are programs put out in Wales, Northern Ireland, the Midlands, and so on. All these places want to do more, theoretically, and the Scottish office of the BBC is a great empire living up in Glasgow. But the Scots have to see these programs at the expense of seeing the regular network programs, and mostly they don't want to give up 'Kojak' or 'Hedda Gabler' in order to see some porky Scots comedy. They want both, but we can't afford both. In Wales it's even more difficult because of the Welsh language, but they get about eight hours a week too.

"One very big difference between your television and ours is the way they're financed. One of our organizations, Independent Television, is financed by advertising. The two BBC networks are financed by a license. What you pay is nine pounds a year for black and white, and eighteen pounds for color. We've got a big population. I don't know how many sets, but enough to bring in 160 million pounds a year. But each household pays one license, no matter how many sets it's got; even if you've got eighteen sets you only pay one license. The system goes back to 1923, when Parliament agreed that radio could be financed in this way, and they've never changed it since.

"But the money doesn't go to the chancellor of the Exchequer, it goes to the post office, which collects it for us, not as agent for the government, but as our agent — at a cost to us of 11 million pounds a year, which even at such a price is cheaper than it would be for us to collect it ourselves, because they've got offices everywhere, you see.

"Actually, it's quite a tricky thing to collect the license. You do it in three ways. First, by straightforward reminders: 'You have not paid this and if you do not pay the attorney general will send you to prison.' The second thing is that we have these absurd vans going around, all green with BBC written all over them. They're absolutely useless, but everybody thinks they can tell whether there's a television set in the house. What the police used to do to homosexuals, we now do to television sets. So we had a big problem till about ten years ago. But when color television came in, most people stopped owning their own sets and started renting them instead, because if they broke down it was easier to get them mended than if they owned them. So you could then arrange with the rental people for the license from the beginning.

"I don't know how many homes have television sets today, but I do know that 94 percent have BBC 1 and 92 percent have BBC 2.

"When that money comes in we have nothing whatsoever to do with it — it's a very curious housekeeping operation — except to set up whatever it is you have to set up to make programs. That is to say, we invest none of it except in our equipment. By now we've got 300 million pounds worth of capital equipment, and studios and film stages and offices and designers. We've got 120 carpenters, and so on. So in a way you can say all that money is spent on programs, directly or indirectly, since some of it goes to the carpenters and some of it comes to me. And I have nothing to do except get up an organization and provide it with a tone, a climate, that moves into the programs that it makes.

"The transmitters are ours as well, though we do have line charges to the post office — a pain in the neck, and I can't tell you how much they cost — because we microwave from our headquarters to a locality, and the post office feeds it to homes, some by lines and some by microwave.

"We have 266 transmitters, 12 of them very large, about 80 medium-sized, and the rest small. That's not counting the things you have for putting up and down valleys. About one quarter of our television sets are fed by cable, but our transmitters do not redirect the signal by cable. We use it for a very different reason, for rediffusion. The cable carries what has been transmitted from our central transmitters to the regional transmitters. This is because of the valleys and because in some parts of the Midlands it's easier to carry by cable. It's also because of an awful lot of rebuilding, and all new towns have the signal brought by cable so they don't have all these antennae knocking about. This is a purely esthetic consideration. Cable in our country is purely a distributive system, and carries no programs of its own making.

"The BBC is a gigantic organization, and by four o'clock in the afternoon the news people are up to here in disaster on celluloid. We have correspondents in Delhi, Paris, Washington, and all over the place. We've got stringers everywhere. We've got the EBU, the European Broadcasting Union, which is actually a news center. And at four o'cock in the afternoon the news editors in Berlin, Amsterdam, Rome, Vienna, and

London all sit down. They talk on a tie line, and among them decide what stories to put out that night as lead stories. We've got satellites too, so that by six o'clock, when we begin to put the news together, we could put on a three-hour bulletin.

"But we don't have time for a three-hour bulletin. On BBC 1 we have a fifteen-minute bulletin early in the evening, and a twenty-five-minute news bulletin at nine o'clock. And on BBC 2 we do it the other way around. On each network we do forty minutes of straight news — what we call bulletins — a night. And ITV does about the same.

"Besides the bulletins we have 'Public Affairs,' two fifty-minute programs at six o'clock and half-past ten. They discuss the news, comment on it. The bulletins are quite separate. There's a great controversy about this. Everybody believes what they hear on the BBC, and we, that is a lot of us in Britain and at the BBC, think it is because we keep the news and the comment strictly separate. A lot of people would like to be like the Walter Cronkite thing, news but also comment and argument about it all mixed in. It's a great issue. I happen to be on the conservative side myself. The reason we separated is that nothing matters about the news except that it is accurate and that it is believed. Comment is something else again.

"We don't have editorials in the sense you do. An editorial is a very tricky thing at the BBC, because we're not owned by separate proprietors, like a newspaper. The way we get around that is quite complicated, but it's elegant and attractive too. On any big issue, until it gets close to legislation, we allow the rapids to run on both sides. For example, take capital punishment, a big issue ten years or so ago, but a simple one. I mean either you hang people or you don't. We had lots of programs about it, and stacks of letters — too many of them. Some people were saying how dreadful it would be to take life, and others how dreadful not to. We had plays written by people who believed in capital punishment and plays written by people who didn't. There was one thing that was important, and that was that it should not be possible for any member of a reasonable group of people, such as this group, to say after six months of programming or so, that the BBC is clearly on one side or the other. So when it came near time for the second reading of the bill in the House, we put on a program about capital punishment that lasted seventy-five minutes. I remember it well because I was director of documentaries at the time and had a lot to do with it. A fellow called Tony de Locbinière directed it, a very good director, and he made it a responsible, proper, many-sided program. But the point is that it would have been impossible to tell from that program whether he was for capital punishment or against it. The main good it did was that it left people on both sides a little better informed. That's not exactly editorializing as newspapers do it or as your TV does it, but it's as near as we got.

"In the handling of local and neighborhood news, I don't think we're as good as you are. On the main networks we have what we call 'Open Door,' which runs about an hour and a half a week, based entirely on the way you do such things in Boston. We think we should have more such programs locally, but not on local networks, and local broadcasting is very difficult for us because the European airways are so crowded. What with Holland and France and Germany and Italy, they all want these airways. And they've all got their defense bands and taxi bands, army bands and every other kind of band. So a station in, say, Liverpool or Edinburgh, which is confined to Liverpool or Edinburgh, is not very easy for us. It's a lot easier in the States. So we have very little local television, whether it's news or any other kind. We hope to improve, but it won't be easy. And it will never be as much as you have here.

"As to television for children, we have absolutely definite

policies about that. Fundamentally — more fundamentally than anything else — we believe that all programs should be good of their type. Whether it's a detective program or a cops and robbers program or a Shakespeare program or a musical, it should be good of that type. So that if the kids choose to watch the damn thing for five hours a day, in the end they're no worse off because the things they've seen are all good of their type, even if they're comics. Mind you, if children watch too much, or too much of one thing, it's like doing anything else too much. I don't want them to watch nothing but sports, or nothing but comics.

"There are special requirements for children from five or six to about twelve. After that children are only little adults, and what they want then is the equivalent of 'Kojak' and 'The Man from U.N.C.L.E.,' and 'All in the Family' — the British equivalent, that is. For the ones younger than twelve we need special sorts of programs, and we do have a very definite children's hour. That's what we call it, only it's more like two hours. The morning, on the whole, is taken up with school stuff, and we put on programs generally called 'Playschool' then and partly in the afternoon. These are for children under five. For the same age group we have something called 'Watch with Mother.' These are very good programs. Then in the afternoon there are various things, and beginning at half-past four, when the children come home from school, we put on children's programs till quarter to six, when the news comes on.

"There's a whole children's department that makes these programs. And they are very, very good programs, and the kids adore them — until they are about twelve, when they want to see grown-up programs. But until then they come home and watch 'Blue Peter,' 'Jack and Orey,' 'Vision On,' which are all enormously popular programs. And we have lots of plays. We do *Kenilworth, Heidi, The Red Shoes,* and all those things. Then between six and eleven o'clock we don't have anything designed just for children, but we have brilliant programs on marvelously adjusted bases, which I would be proud and pleased for any child of mine to see at any time. The fact, of course, is that half of them are rotten, because we don't make them well enough. But the intention is that they should be as good as we can make them on their own terms.

"As for the 'mindless cartoons' you worry about on television in this country, I can't honestly say our kids get much of that, either on BBC or on the independent network. What they like most is plays. Of course, I dare say that if we had a channel at home that was nothing but cartoons, we'd find the children watching the cartoons. If you put on cartoon after cartoon, they'd watch, I'd think. After all, kids go for the soft option like everybody else.

"We don't have much violence, either. Plenty of sex on the BBC, but not much violence.

"The BBC is not an educational network, in any sense like the one you've got here. It doesn't think of programs as being educational. Programs are to provide two things, either insight or delight. If they provide insight, that's nice. If they provide delight, that's nice. And if they provide both, that's great. But they're not there to educate, or do anything like it, in any formal sense. The kind of educating they do is general and pervasive, not overt. And remember what I said this afternoon. Our programs are written by writers, not by committees, and by the best writers we can get. If we want a play we go to Pinter, and if we want economics we go to Galbraith, always the best we can get. We don't always care whether a program is a 'pop' program or a 'good' program, though we are always aware of the difference. But we do always care, and we care very very much, that as far as we can make it, it must be good of its own kind."

4

New Politics and Old Values

GEORGE MCGOVERN

The candidate who carried Massachusetts in the presidential election of 1972 spoke to a full and enthusiastic house at New England Life Hall when he addressed the Bicentennial Forums late in January 1976. He took a broad view of the social, economic, political, and international problems of the day, but occasionally zoomed in on particulars such as the tax structure, welfare, Watergate, and the repercussions of the Vietnam war. His theme was reform within the framework of our democratic idea-structure shaped by a reapplication of our national ideals.

One of our leading liberals, George McGovern has represented South Dakota in the Senate since 1962. Before that he was a member of the House of Representatives and a special assistant to President Kennedy. In World War II he was decorated with the Distinguished Flying Cross. After earning a Ph.D. at Northwestern, he returned to his alma mater, Dakota Wesleyan University, as a professor of history. He is the author of War Against Want, Agricultural Thought in the Twentieth Century, A Time of War/A Time of Peace, The Great Coalfield War *(with L. F. Guttridge), and* An American Journey.

IN THIS BICENTENNIAL PERIOD we celebrate not just the date of the nation's becoming, but the very reason of our national being. And we must bind America anew to the revolutionary meaning of its birth and the best moments of our national history.

Our forebears achieved progress because they conceived of this country as a process to be perfected, not a piece of property to be used or abused by each passing generation. What they declared in 1776 was not the fullness of American freedom, but the common privilege that we all share of laboring for the fulfillment of that promise; and that task, as we know, is never finally completed.

Each generation has its own summons to life, liberty, and the pursuit of happiness.

In the first century of our national existence, our forebears made a constitution and tamed a continent. They engaged each other in civil war to secure the union and the emancipation of another race.

In the second century of our history, Americans shaped a further revolution of industry, science, invention, and abundance, and shared its wonders with the rest of the world. Woodrow Wilson and Franklin Roosevelt both spoke of a peace without victory, and they dreamed of an international organization that would be strong enough to discipline national rivalry and greed.

Of course, any fair chronicle of American deeds must record violations of our ideals — the oppression of women and children at various times in our history, the bitter lash of racial and ethnic prejudice, the ravaging of the precious resources and environment, ill-conceived and tragic ventures abroad, and other regrets of our national past.

And yet, the encouraging aspect of all this is that, invariably, Americans themselves have sooner or later called their country to account. My own generation struggled out of perhaps the worst depression in our national experience. We fought a valiant and victorious battle with world Fascism. In more recent years, blacks and whites have marched together in this country for civil justice. And finally we broke out of the mire of Vietnam, perhaps the darkest chapter in 200 years of national experience. We did that more because of the force of free dissent among ourselves than the firepower that was arrayed against us.

The sustaining basis of this democracy is that when we have become lost in the wilds of injustice and deceit and wrongdoing, it is our own first ideals that have ultimately beckoned us home. That call is harder for us to discern in this Bicentennial period, when we are uncertain of what our duty is or of what we can accomplish.

After the waste of a war that was as long as it was wrong, after a leadership of lying and lawbreaking, in the midst of economic disarray, the words of Thomas Paine are once again relevant: "These are the times that try men's souls."

To this present crisis of national spirit we must respond as he did: to declare the American Revolution — not as a routine phrase of an anniversary year, not as another political slogan without substance, but as a commitment to constructive change so that we may continue to specify and apply in these times the principles of those earlier trying times.

We must, in Lincoln's phrase, "think anew, and act anew." Nor can those who would lead a struggle to build a new politics based on the renewal of old values wait for easy public acceptance. The work of leadership is the willingness to stand and fight for what is decent and just even before it is perceived by a majority. That is what I think many Americans attempted to do in 1972 and what we must do again and again in the years ahead.

We won a presidential nomination in 1972 and then lost a presidential election. But our course was right, despite any tactical mistakes that were made, in both phases of the struggle. We introduced the practice and have now gained ac-

69

ceptance of the principle that our politics should be financed
and directed by the many — not controlled by the few. That
is now the law of the land in this country. We offered an alternative to an economy that was painfully distorted by in-
flated and excessive arms, and that alternative, or something
like it, must be accepted if we are to break free from the
wastes, the distortions, and the inflation that go with a war
economy of the kind that has gripped us for so many years.

We offered a reconstruction of taxes and the maintenance of
income for the poor and the weak that is based on justice and
compassion. And that reconstruction must one day soon re-
place a tax structure that is geared too much to those that are
privileged and a welfare system that by any test fails us all.

Above all, we forced an end to a terrible war in Indochina,
the scene of which I have visited in the last few days.

Much remains to be done. The works of peace and justice
are never finished, as every thoughtful person knows, but I
have no doubt that the essential goals of what we attempted to
accomplish in 1972 will be achieved at some future time in our
American experience.

We must declare again the liberty of the American economy.
We know that our ancestors rebelled against a foreign domin-
ion over their earnings and commerce. We commemorate
them best and serve ourselves better by resisting a domination
no less alien simply because it comes from within. They proclaimed: No taxation without representation. We must demand: No taxation without justice.

The Americans of 1776 defied the Loyalists of tyranny; the
Americans of 1976 must take on the lobbyists of privilege.
That struggle may be a matter of many years, as it was at the
beginning of our country. But let it be a Bicentennial resolve
that we shall reach the point in this nation where no worker
will pay a higher portion of income for taxes than is paid by
the wealthy. This does not mean the division of society, of
class against class, but the unity of every American of every

status, each in giving a fair amount to the support of self-government. Only then can we resume the oldest of our national efforts: to increase the meaning and measure of liberty in the lives of our people.

In order to free millions of our families from a forced neglect of illness and unaffordable costs of treatment, we must have fair taxation to finance and deliver adequate health care. If that is done fairly, it will be an investment that the American people will gladly finance. In order to free a portion of our population from despair, we must have fair taxation to guarantee employment for all who can work and minimal income for those unable to work. Just as the colonists had to win their freedom from a king who scorned their petitions, so we must widen the writ of freedom in the face of entrenched privilege in our own society.

I think we have either to dissolve or discipline more effectively than we have in the past the great economic concentrations that raise the price and reduce the standard of living of our people. Persistent inflation robs the people of their earnings and it undermines the economic foundations that are essential to a free society. I do not believe it is possible for freedom to continue indefinitely in a society in the grip of double-digit inflation. We must undo a military-industrial complex that lavishes our resources on excessive weapons, weakens our prosperity by useless production, and wagers the peace on an arms race that can only lead to greater danger and degradation for us all.

The needs of a continuing American Revolution are indivisible: we cannot meet some and set others aside because they are more complicated or more inconvenient. Our ancestors found that they could not trade with all nations so long as they were a colony in one empire. For us, the cost of military overkill or an unjust tax deduction is that those lost revenues deny work to the jobless, health care to the sick, and an end to the pollution of our neighborhoods.

71

Now there are limits, of course, to what government can do. It is true that neither this society nor more specifically our government can do everything. But it is a deception to argue that we cannot become anything very different or very much better than what we have been in the recent past.

New priorities and more humane policies have been the hope of the past decade. They have guided the dialogue through most of the years that I have been in public life. But they must become the pledge and the proof of an authentic Bicentennial. They alone can lay the foundation of a revolution for further liberty — liberty that frees us from the grip of militarism and monopoly, and from the more nearly ultimate tyranny that faces so many of our people in the form of malnutrition, joblessness, and untreated disease.

As we seek to enrich our freedom, we must prevent the erosion of first and fundamental rights that we used to take for granted. It is a sad but essential thing that we find it necessary to affirm again that first Bill of Rights. But in the end liberty is sustained as it was secured at the start — by the votes and the vigilance of our citizens. Government will be no better than what we expect of it, and it often will be as bad as we are willing to accept. Public officials may disdain conscience or disobey the Constitution, but politicians do follow the election returns. Adlai Stevenson believed, as I believe, that we get the kind of government we deserve by our own vigilance and our own wisdom. So by our votes and our own vigilance there are certain principles that we need to hold to be self-evident now:

First of all, that it is the truth that makes us free — that in a democracy, no campaign, and especially one for the presidency, and no foreign policy, especially one that involves the waging of war, can justify the telling of lies to the people and their elected representatives. It is an outrage that, almost before the smoke of the Vietnam war was cleared away, our leaders had the temerity to involve us secretly in another civil war, thousands of miles away from our shores, in Angola.

Government is supposed to listen to Americans, not to listen in on them; the White House should not be a den of eavesdroppers, the FBI should not be an agent of blackmail, and law and order are not kept by committing crimes.

It should be self-evident that tax returns should be a method of reporting income to the government, not a means of intimidating and punishing the opposition. I regret to say that many substantial contributors to my 1972 campaign had mysterious tax audits in the months since that election.

Who among us would dare to deny these essential principles to which I have referred — which should be as obvious to Americans as they are ancient to our tradition? Most people, at least for the time being, give their reverence to them now, because we have gone through a painful experience in recent months where we have seen, to our sorrow, the hazards of a politics unguided by moral and constitutional principles.

And there will be a next time, when we will once again be tempted to distrust each other's patriotism, to suspect each other for our diversity of color and convictions, of age and accents, or even of our dress and music. That time may come again in this Bicentennial, because this is another election year, a time that could become an occasion to exploit racial fear, economic insecurity, and international danger. So let us celebrate the Revolution, not desecrate its most sacred values: let us reject easy deceptions, irrelevant issues, and promises that are made to be broken.

The rights of Americans are a seamless web. The strand that ties them together in a democratic society, that is trampled underfoot by standing in schoolhouse doors or killing Asian and Latin revolutionaries, is the same invisible strand that secures the doors of an office in Watergate — or of a home in South Boston. It is not possible to observe the law part of the time, when it is convenient, and to desecrate it when it does not serve our own purpose. Many times we will find rulings that do not serve our convenience, but if the rule of law, and the claims of decency, are subordinated to our own convenience, then no one of us can ever again be secure in our possessions and in our rights. That is why it is so important to honor the rule of law in this society.

It has always been a matter of interest to me that Thomas Jefferson wanted to be remembered not for the high political offices that he held but for his authorship of the Declaration of Independence, the Virginia Statute on religious liberty, and the University of Virginia. Like Jefferson, we must value first principles above winning by expediency or the holding of any office of politics. There would not have been a Declaration of Independence by Jefferson and his colleagues had it not been for the wellspring of the Judeo-Christian ethic that preceded it by many hundreds of years. Today we cannot renew the American spirit without reaffirming the moral underpinning of our society and our politics.

As we seek to form what we call a more perfect union among ourselves, we must also assume a more appropriate place among the powers of the earth. We have been taught in terrible tragedy a truth that should have been self-evident: that freedom is not something that we can force upon others at our own time and choosing. They will choose their own definition of freedom, or their own vision of what their future ought to be. That is their right — and it is not our capacity or our responsibility.

"A decent respect for the opinions of mankind" requires recognition that for masses of people around the globe the names of Marx and Lenin, Mao and Chou, Ho Chi Minh and Madame Binh, Castro and Che Guevara, Lumumba and Nyerere, no matter what they evoke in our consciousness, evoke for others those images of patriotism and high purpose that come to us at the mention of Washington and Adams, Jefferson and Madison. The proper goal for us is not a world molded in the American image, but in President Kennedy's perceptive phrase, "A world made safe for diversity." And

74

this requires both the strength of humility and a generous measure of restraint on our part at a time when we have great power.

We cannot pay any price, no matter how much: we cannot reach every goal, no matter how minor. America must be known no longer as a gunrunner to dictators, a bomber of villages, a plotter of coups.

This great and good land has values to offer that go far beyond our firepower or our material wealth. The manipulators of power warn that a foreign policy of principle is not practical. But another decade of expediency over principle and I think we will be undone as a great force in the world.

Neither interventionists nor isolationists, let us be internationalists, protecting the legitimate interests of our security and pursuing the indispensable interests of the human family. We have a vital stake in the security of Western Europe and the Pacific Sea. We have an essential role in making and maintaining a settlement in the Middle East. We could flee those obligations only at our own peril.

We have the most basic interest in détente with both the Soviet Union and the people of China, whatever their mutual hostility toward each other and our separate disputes with either of them. To link détente with lesser issues is to hazard Armageddon for the sake of an Angola.

And in this hemisphere which is our home, and toward that half of the planet that is still ill-housed, ill-clad, and ill-fed, let us follow our own decent traditions instead of imitating the worst instincts and practices of others. When we are tempted to match the heavy foot of others in emerging Africa, let us recall that those who tread too roughly invite their own rejection and isolation.

America's strength lies in the infection of our ideals and in the sharing of our resources and techniques. We have 6 percent of the earth's population. We hold 30 percent of its

75

wealth. Yet, today we contribute less than a quarter of 1 percent of our national product to the development of the poor around this planet.

We must reduce our foreign aid of weapons designed to control people, and increase technical aid to help bring under control the teeming population growth. We must send plowshares for farming instead of spending resources for payoffs to corrupt regimes. With vivid images of a tour over the last three weeks that took me through the slums of Calcutta and Dacca and the villages of Pakistan and India, I am aware again of the awesome gap of existence between us and them. Far too many of them may live or die by bread alone, because the blunt facts are, in those parts of the world, that there are too many people and there is too little bread.

Their condition threatens our own. I do not believe that the world can permanently continue partly in prosperity and mostly in poverty. The cost of their despair will be continuing international terror and instability. So morality and prudence, as they sometimes do, merge in commanding the endeavors of development: having enough to spare, we have an obligation to share.

The true spirit of America is to be honest about these realities with ourselves and with our fellow Americans. The admission of a mistake is the first condition of its correction. I would like to say here again that I still believe one act above all else would signal a return to the ideals of our Revolution: not a begrudging and conditional pardoning of our war resisters, who were right, but unconditional readmission to their country, which was in the wrong. I don't think there's much to be accomplished at this late date in the history of the Vietnam chapter in attempting to belabor the sins or the guilt of any one individual, but certainly least of all should our anger and our punishment be directed at those young men who followed their conscience into exile or into prison.

Amnesty takes on new force when we consider that a President has been pardoned by a successor who still does not understand the real meaning of amnesty as it relates to the Vietnam struggle.

But the reconciliation between those who opposed the war and those who supported it must be joined by the reconciliation and reconstruction of Vietnam. Here is a suffering little country that has been bled and torn for almost thirty years at the hands of Japanese, French, and Americans; that is eager, from all surface indications, to establish a rational and peaceful relationship with us and the rest of the world. After the Second World War, a war in which I and millions of others participated, we thought it was in our interest to help reconstruct the Japanese and German nations, who had been our enemies. The question now is whether we can be as magnanimous when we lose as when we win. One fact is clear: we cannot wash away the guilt of our Vietnam tragedy except through the spirit of reconciliation and the works of reconstruction. We shall carry that guilt until we make some positive step in the direction of reconstruction. This is not only in our self-interest, as it was thirty years ago, after World War II, but it is necessary for our souls and for our standing in the eyes of the rest of the human family. We need to pursue that unfinished agenda of Vietnam with the tenacity that many brought to ending the war at an earlier time.

Finally, if a willingness to confront our errors is in the spirit of America, so is a capacity for imagination and innovation always rooted in those simple values of common sense and decency. Our economy is no more fated to decline in 1976 than it was to remain permanently paralyzed in the Depression of the 1930s. But the return of prosperity and peace requires a politics which does not claim a neat set of nostrums — which admits uncertainty and ventures innovation. George Washington lost more battles than he ever won, and so did Abraham Lincoln, and so did Franklin Roosevelt. But in the end they prevailed. And so will we — if we reject disproven assumptions and the groundless fear of innovation. We must at least be willing to consider such reforms as public ownership of certain resources and the building of peace through law.

Half a century ago, Walter Lippmann made this observation:

> We are trying to be too shrewd, too clever, too calculating, when what the anxious and suffering peoples cry out to us for is that we practice the elemental virtues and adhere to the eternal verities. They alone can guide us through the complications of our days . . .

That is what I believe to be the message of the Bicentennial and that is what I believe will give meaning and purpose to our lives.

Questions and Discussion

Senator McGovern was given a long and hearty round of applause, which was perhaps not surprising from a select group in the only state that voted against President Nixon in 1972. But more questions were handed up from the floor than to any other speaker in either series of the Bicentennial Forums, and this seemed more than a pro forma response to an address that was the next thing to a blueprint for liberalism à la 1976.

The questions were rather evenly divided between socioeconomic concerns on the one hand and politics and international relations on the other. Questions of the first kind touched on starvation, inflation, unemployment, a minimum wage, tax reform, health insurance, and how to defeat the lobbies of special privilege. Questions on political problems and international relations ranged from campaign contributions, the possibility of decay in the quality of our national leadership, the growth of presidential power at the expense of Congress, the CIA at home and abroad, the Arab-Israeli conflict pro and con, and above all war and the danger of a conflict that could erupt into World War III. Some of the questioners reflected a genuine agony of indecision between the dangers confronting a helpless nation in the hands of what they saw as a ruthless and self-centered military-industrial complex and the equally frightening consequences of reducing the defense budget in the face of an ever-stronger Russia and an expanding China. The uncertainties of this issue cut more deeply into the thoughts and feelings of this audience than did any other. It was not clear whether Senator McGovern agreed with many of his listeners that this is the gravest issue facing the nation today. But he was generous with his time and full in his answers, and the question period lasted nearly as long as the address.

After dinner at the Parkman House that evening the discussion turned first to Senator McGovern's recent visits to Vietnam, Bangladesh, and India, and his acute observations on those peoples and their problems. He was surprisingly optimistic and hopeful about the future of Vietnam.

It is very interesting, he began, than Hanoi apparently harbors no bitterness toward the United States people as such, even though the North took a terrific pounding during the war. "The aerial bombardment was as heavy as anything we threw against the Germans or the Japanese in World War II, and it fell in a much more restricted area, on a more fragile country. But they blame that on American leadership, not the American people. They don't even show any bitterness toward the forces of General Thieu. They blame a few military opportunists willing to serve the interests of our leaders. They always felt it was Johnson's war, or Nixon's, or whoever was in power, and that sooner or later the best instincts of the American people would take over and the war would end — and that's exactly what happened.

"Unlike the Chinese, who seemed to want isolation after their revolution succeeded in 1949, the Vietnamese are eager to open relations with all countries, particularly the United

States. Of course, they want our aid and help in reconstruction, but beyond that, *I'm* convinced that they don't want to be solely dependent on either the Soviet Union or Peking. They want broad contacts in the international community, and I think it's in our interest to respond.

"Our experience with Cuba argues that we should. We tried to bring down the Cuban regime by embargo, isolation, and so on. It hasn't worked. Instead it has driven the Cubans into a tighter and tighter relationship with Russia. Ours was a self-defeating policy. So today we have the Cubans in Angola, where I don't think they would be if we'd had normal relations with them in recent years. Who is to say what will happen in Vietnam if the only place they can turn for help is the Communist world? They're Communists themselves, in their own way, but Vietnam nationalists first and foremost. It's probably true that the rank and file couldn't care less about politics. What they want is a roof over their heads and a chance to make a living and take care of their families.

"I asked three or four Northern leaders what was the secret of their victory over us. They said it was the fact they had an unchanging purpose, national independence, and freedom from foreign domination. They had all the national chips on their side, the patriotic fervor of those who had fought the Japanese, then the French, and now us, whereas the South had as leaders only lackeys in foreign pay. The Vietnamese people want a free and independent country, but when they say this they aren't talking about freedom of the press or freedom to criticize the government. They want freedom to take care of their families and freedom from foreign domination."

Asked about other Far Eastern countries he visited, Senator McGovern said he could not be optimistic about Bangladesh, but that India had made progress in the fifteen years since he last saw it, and that Pakistan also showed signs of progress. But Bangladesh, he said, "seemed nothing short of an economic disaster. The country has the incredible paradox of a

250-inch annual rainfall, with alternating floods and droughts. They have worked out no way to conserve this fantastic amount of water and to save it for the dry season. They have three or four crops a year, two or three of which burn up, while the other floods out. They also have very little control of population growth. They are already the eighth biggest country in the world, with something like 90 million people! Direct shipments of food from us won't help them much, except in a very temporary way. They need technical help from our agricultural experts, engineers, and water resources people. But whether or not their leadership has the vision to use this help wisely is open to question. A lot of their best people have been killed off, including Raman, the man who led the independence movement. He and his whole family were assassinated a few months ago, and the President convinces you in fifteen minutes' talk that he shouldn't be running a village, let alone a country. Pakistan is taking a certain satisfaction in their troubles, and India seems to want a subservient government in Bangladesh that looks to the Indians for control. I don't know whether they're going to make it or not.

"Both India and Pakistan have strong and dynamic, though authoritarian, leadership, and the danger of war between them has diminished. But our relations with India have deteriorated as those with Bangladesh have improved, and the immense amount of aid we have given India since World War II is now having very little effect on their attitude toward us. India is also afraid of China, and our closer relations with China aren't helping us with India but are moving her closer to Russia. Mrs. Gandhi talks about the external threat, and has recently charged that the United States through the CIA is buying up newspapers and trying to subvert her government. Our ambassador, William Saxbe, who has been pro-India and who asked for the assignment, has handled the matter well. He called Colby and Kissinger and threatened to resign if these charges were true, and was assured by both of them that they were not. He told this to Mrs. Gandhi bluntly, and she admitted that she had no real evidence, but said that the U.S. record in Chile, Vietnam, and elsewhere was such that one could presume that we were doing the same things in India. That," said Senator McGovern, "is what she told me — that her only evidence was circumstantial."

Late in January 1976, at the time of this discussion, the congressional investigation of the CIA was at its height, and it was inevitable that the topic be raised. Senator McGovern said he had felt for a long time that the agency's function should be limited to the gathering of information and intelligence. That was its original purpose, not the subversion of elections and all the rest. He thought there was no need for Congress to have access to all the information gathered by the CIA. Congress should know what the agency is doing, what its function is, and whether it is committing American funds abroad as it was then doing in Angola. "We not only should know when they are doing such things, but we should take steps to curb them." But if they were limited by law to gathering information, that information should go to the Executive Branch, and Congress has no need to be briefed on every bit of information they have on internal developments in other countries. The CIA becomes dangerous when it gets us involved in paramilitary activities, upsetting governments and subverting institutions in other countries. Asked whether he thought Congress would take strong steps to curb the CIA and limit its activities, he said he would not predict what action it would take.

Not surprisingly the question of desegregation and the busing of schoolchildren came up, but in the interesting context of what works in government and what does not. Senator McGovern said he thought sometimes we give up too quickly on problems, and commented that the first court-ordered busing was in Charlotte, North Carolina, a city now at peace, where busing has been a unifying experience. It has also worked well in Prince Georges County outside Washington, and in many other places. If in some places it does not yet seem to be working, people should not give up.

It was pointed out that busing has not worked well in Boston, and the question was raised whether five years from now we would be saying that the people of South Boston had been right in resisting, just as we now say many resisters to the draft were right during the Vietnam war. To this the senator answered that he never favored amnesty for anyone while we were still at war and would not advocate disobeying the law on busing as long as it was in effect. But he did not believe that now we should be punishing people who had stood up against the war. Similarly with busing, as long as the court orders to use the process are in effect, people may be free to protest them, but they are not free to ignore them and set them aside. They can appeal to a higher court, but there comes a point where the Supreme Court finally rules, and when you reach that ultimate stage, there is no recourse but to obey the law, unless you are willing to go to jail.

The discussion of busing, particularly in Boston, led to the most interesting topic of the evening. How well do we know, how carefully do we examine what works in government, what will work, and what will not? The questioner recalled our Cuban policy in the last decade, and why it had not worked. And he mentioned the present turmoil over busing in Boston, which has certainly not worked. For every piece of legislation, he surmised, there must be economic limits, psychological limits, and social limits to what is possible and practicable, and he wondered whether our government at the present time is always aware of what will work and what will not work, and may indeed sometimes be acting counterproductively.

Senator McGovern answered promptly that he thought there is more willingness today to look at that problem than there has been at any time since he has been in government, greater sensitivity to the fact that government is limited in what it can do. He felt that there is less optimism about major federal programs and what they can do, but he also warned against the dangers of carrying that trend too far. He said that when New York City got into trouble there wasn't much it could do to pull out of it purely by its own resources. Federal help was essential, and nearly everybody who lived in the city, however much he may have cursed Washington, realized the need. This realization was the only hope of salvation, and it came about because people on all sides were concerned with the question of what would work and what would not.

At this point an administrative assistant to the mayor of Boston brought up a related problem; that while we have been successful in bringing issue-consciousness into American politics, we have been less successful in implementing the general objectives once we have conceived them. In Congress general objectives in the form of legislation are passed on to a bureaucratic organization that is not structured to carry out those objectives. After issues are debated in the legislature, and objectives are adopted, the administrative bureaucracy that is supposed to put all this into effect becomes so complicated in dealing with state and local governments that by the time an originally well-stated objective is put into effect, it has been so changed and distorted during transmutation into rules and regulations that it hasn't a chance of succeeding. Either it is adopted as legislation without thought of how it should work, or administrative bureaucracies so complicate it that the original objective is lost sight of in the maze of regulations. We send a perfectly respectable objective through so many layers of government that we totally diffuse accountability and responsibility. Federal, state, and local people ought to sit down together much more frequently than they do. As it is, legislative and administrative branches often lose sight of each other's abilities and objectives, and sometimes seem not to have understood them in the first place. All too often objectives get translated into regulations without being thoroughly understood. Then it becomes the aim merely to carry out the regulations, with little or no regard to the meaning and intent of the original objectives.

Senator McGovern agreed, in light of his own experience in Congress, that there is sometimes such a maze of bureaucratic regulations that a legislative program bogs down of its own weight. As an example he cited the Occupational Health and Safety Act, which had the excellent objective of setting standards for working conditions in order to reduce fire and industrial hazards. Its purpose was to deal with conditions in factories, mines, pollution in large places, etc. "But it was applied to the little Mom and Pop stores on Main Street, where people are given an arbitrary fine of $250 because the fire extinguisher is hanging in the wrong place, or somebody hasn't repaired a leaky spot in the roof. In my state the program became one of harassment, not one to improve working conditions. We were besieged by complaints against picayune regulations. For small businesses particularly the paperwork was enough to drive people to insanity. You have to use common sense in things like that. A few months ago we were trying to get through an amendment to eliminate employers with three or more employees, and Senator Javits asked whether it was less moral to kill people in firms that have ten employees than in those that have only three. But you have to draw the line someplace. There are more accidents at home than on the job, but government can't send inspectors into the home to make sure people have the windows shut and the faucets fixed. No program will work without some measure of common sense."

5

The Third Century and the Third Generation

Daniel P. Moynihan

When the tall, free-swinging former ambassador to the United Nations stepped up to the microphones in Faneuil Hall on February 12, 1976, the atmosphere was electric in more ways than one. The media were out in force. Hall and stage were a clutter of cameras and a dazzle of lights. Moynihan had resigned from the U.N. post a few days before, and this was the day he had returned to teaching at Harvard. The audience was tense with speculation about what he might allow himself to say, and about whom.

But on this vast range of topics he remained tantalizingly untopical. Instead he delivered an almost apocalyptic message, the gist of which was that as our material welfare has improved our people have become steadily less content, that the discontent is "an amalgam of unhappiness" felt by different groups about different things, and that social analysis by Presidential Commission has become progressively less scholarly, less concerned with ultimately human as distinct from economic problems and less clear of vision.

Daniel P. Moynihan, this year elected senator from New York, has served under four Presidents, Kennedy, Johnson, Nixon, and Ford, has been ambassador to India, and has served in NATO and as assistant secretary of labor. He holds degrees from Tufts University and some twenty honorary degrees, and has held various

86

academic posts in urban studies and government at Harvard and M.I.T. Author of several books, he received the 1963 Anisfield-Wolf Award in Race Relations for Beyond the Melting Pot *(with Nathan Glazer).*

THE GULF of perception that sometimes separates academe from the other world came to me rather vividly ten days ago when I called the dean of Harvard College and said, "Mr. Dean, I am calling to tell you that I have sent my resignation to the President." The dean said, "I am terribly disappointed to hear that." And I said, "Well, so am I really, but I just don't feel I can stay here." And he said, "Oh, you mean *that* President."

With an effort to make that adjustment, I began by recalling a letter that John Adams wrote to his wife, Abigail, in 1780, in which he observed that it was his duty to study the science of government more than all other sciences. In his view, for his time, the arts of legislation and administration and negotiation ought to take the place of, indeed to exclude in a manner, all other arts. "I must study politics and war that my sons may have liberty to study mathematics and philosophy. My sons ought to study mathematics and philosophy, geography, natural history, naval architecture, navigation, commerce and agriculture in order to give their children the right to study painting, poetry, music, architecture, statuary, tapestry, and porcelain."

One wonders how much Adams would approve of the extraordinary fulfillment of his vision. Surely he would have hoped for some carryover of the disciplines of sterner times; at one time recently, at what he called "our University of Cambridge," the proportion of graduates proposing to enter commerce dropped to 5½ percent.

Yet, most of us today would acknowledge a movement of politics away from the concerns of the first two generations of

Adamses, if we may use that image, toward the concerns of the third generation as we enter this third century, at least among those Americans who can be thought of as inheriting a measure of substance and tradition from their past.

This appears to be a change in our national life and poses the challenge to government that any change will do. On this score, it is perhaps well to recall a not less prophetic observation of Adams in a letter to Jefferson of 1813. "While all other sciences have advanced," he wrote, "that of government is at a stand, little better understood, little better practiced now than three or four thousand years ago; for there is no question but that a little-advanced government is being asked by a much-advanced citizenry to concern itself increasingly with that most elusive of all possible public questions: the quality of life."

"Quality," said the physicist Ernest Rutherford, "is nothing but poor quantification."

Some who speak of the quality of life will very likely find in such a statement just those aspects of modern society that concern them: a seemingly pervasive materialism, a Philistine denial of spiritual and esthetic values, as evidenced in, well, the quality of things. And yet, what spiritual and esthetic achievement has the modern age witnessed more splendid than that of nuclear physics, an achievement preceded, accompanied, and followed by meticulous, painstaking measurements.

This point acquires further salience when it is recalled that Rutherford was talking about the term "quality" as applied to physical phenomena. In the early history of modern science, the term was much in use, to explain, one fears, that which could not otherwise be explained. In time, of course, more specific, more quantifiable concepts took over, and yet the term ought not to be discarded. When, for example, we read in William James that the alpha and omega of a university is the tone of it and this tone is set by human personalities exclusively, we know what he means, and we may reflect that the qualitative term he uses here — "tone" — is susceptible to exact quantification when applied to music, and so why not in other matters?

Obviously we are groping here, but just as obviously, we are on to something. When in the life of individuals and the community of nations a longing appears, an unease, a dissatisfaction with things as they are, it is fair to assume that something may be changing with respect to fundamental orientations. Long-settled patterns of motivation may be shifting; people may be changing their minds — an event that doesn't happen often, but does nonetheless happen. To the strength of democratic government, one reason ours now approaches its Bicentennial is that when this does happen, social arrangements usually can change also; so that after a period of mounting disequilibrium, a new stability emerges. Something of this order appears to be taking place in the United States, whilst remarkably recent developments appear in other industrial democracies, such that the impression grows that cultural, rather than merely political, forces are abroad.

The concept of postindustrial society advanced by Daniel Bell is the most elaborate effort yet made to encompass these changes within a general theory. Predictably, postindustrial society comes to question the preoccupation with economic growth, which characterized its predecessor. If this is not predictable, it may be said to be logical. There are trade-offs between the acquisition of material goods and the acquisition of other goods.

Leisure, as an example, which individuals once freed from what Marx called the "realm of necessity," deals all the while with these trade-offs while seeking to "maximize" a mix of things of which producing goods and services is but one component. As with individuals, so with society. The question now is how much government growth also arises, albeit the answers differ.

That the growth of government should be an issue, if not necessarily predictable, certainly was predicted. From Aldous Huxley to George Orwell, the spread of government regulation into what de Tocqueville called the "minor details of life" has been part of the prophetic vision of the modern age. But where the first question is much discussed, the second is not. In part, this may arise from the issue of big government having been too much discussed at a time when government was anything but big. In part, it arises also from the seeming tendency of those who would restrict economic growth to turn to government, and hence to government growth, to bring this about. In general, the tendency of those who would change America for the better is to seek to do so through an increase in government, even though it is often the aftermath of previous increases in government that are the conditions it hoped to change. If this proposition is correct, and to the extent that it is, there is at least a modest hope that social science may help to clarify matters and even contribute to some resolution.

In 1932, the Committee on Recent Social Trends, submitting its report to President Hoover, remarked that it did not wish to exaggerate the role of intelligence in social direction. Neither should we. The Committee's assessment of the situation then seems to hold for the present also. "Social action," it wrote, "is the resultant of many forces, among which, in an age of science and education, conscious intelligence may certainly be reckoned as one but one force only, and in no way the most important."

Still, it is a defensible belief, based on American experience, that a conscious and hopefully intelligent effort to learn what is bothering us could provide some marginal assistance in what appears to be an incipient revolution of a sort, using the term "revolution" as the founders of the American Republic would originally have understood it; that is, as a turning of the circle to a new position, showing forth a different range of principles and preferences in a still-joined and harmonious whole. Conscious intelligence may help us to discern what these new preferences and principles may be, and if we do that, we can expect some success with the task of measuring the quality of life as a prelude to improving it. Perhaps we shall have some success.

A severe modesty is required as one approaches a subject this large and ill-defined. Certainly, presidential efforts of this order have shown a formidable decline in quality over the past two generations. During this span of time, three Presidents have undertaken systematic inquiries into the state of the nation, with respect to large matters of shifting values and judgments, as well as of changing conditions. As this is an activity widely and reasonably not associated with national planning, it is not without interest that each of the three, President Hoover, President Eisenhower, and President Nixon, was thought by his contemporaries to be more on the conservative side of issues than otherwise, a fact that at least suggests that the correspondence between an interest in centralized economic direction and a comparable interest in comprehensive social assessment is not as strong as it is routinely assumed.

But more noteworthy is the decline in quality. The first effort, that of President Hoover, resulted in a major, scholarly, indeed intellectual, achievement; the formidable two-volume report *Recent Social Trends*. It was accompanied by an equally distinguished series of monographs on specific subjects. Almost three decades later, President Eisenhower's Commission on National Goals issued its study, *Goals for Americans*, a thoroughly competent and at points distinguished study, but if such a comparison may be admitted, a quarter the size of the earlier effort and with but little associated schaolarship. A decade after that, the first report of President Nixon's National Goals Research Staff's *Toward Balanced Growth: Quantity with*

Quality, if not without redeeming features, appeared almost as a fugitive publication in a government setting profoundly suspicious of its essentially undemanding prescriptions.

Too much can be inferred from a sequence of unrelated government reports, and yet, one is impressed by the decline in competence in the sense of potential mastery to be sensed in these studies. This is all the more striking in view of the settings in which the successive reports emerged. *Recent Social Trends* appeared at the depth of the worst economic depression in American history. The inarticulate misery of the hundreds of thousands or millions of breadwinners who were deprived of their livelihoods through no fault of their own is acknowledged throughout the text, but it has not made miserable men or women of the authors. In part, this equipoise arose from the laissez-faire assignment they had undertaken. They wrote, "We were not commissioned to lead the people into some new land of promise, but to retrace our recent wanderings, to indicate and interpret our ways and rates of change, to provide maps of progress, make observations of danger zones, point out hopeful roads of advance, be helpful in finding a more intelligent course in the next phase of our progress."

Appointed in the autumn of 1929, it submitted its report three years later. In his foreword, President Hoover, weeks away from defeat by Franklin D. Roosevelt, noted with laconic indirection, "Since the task assigned to the Committee was to inquire into changing trends, the result is emphasis on elements of instability, rather than stability, in our social structure."

In truth, the Committee came close to writing the agenda of the New Deal: a change in the distribution of income, a solvent employment fund, social insurance, economic planning. The report pointed to the anomalies of American life: splendid technical proficiency in some incredible skyscraper and monstrous backwardness in some equally incredible slum. It dealt with just those general subjects that would take up so much of

American life in the generations that followed: minority groups, labor in society, women, public welfare, social work, schools, medicine, crime, and the growth of governmental functions. Some of its concerns would at first recede in interest in the years that followed, and then come forward once again: ethnic groups and immigration policies, rural trends and problems, the arts, and corruption and ineffectiveness of much of our governmental machinery.

Whatever else the Committee's report achieved, it certainly demonstrated that "conscious intelligence" (its term) can make an impressive judgment as to what is going to be bothering a country for a half century to come. "Poverty," the Committee noted, "is by no means vanquished. Even during the late period of unexampled prosperity, there was much poverty in certain industries and localities, in rural areas as well as in cities, which was not of a temporary or accidental nature."

In the midst of the Depression, the task at hand was to regain our former standards, but the longer and greater task — to achieve standards that are socially acceptable — will remain.

Recent Social Trends was remarkable for many things, not least for the candor and clarity with which the Committee set forth at the outset its conviction that science and technology, the work of the second Adams generation, was the primary source of the social trends it was tracing. The automobile affects the railroad, the family, the size of cities, the types of crimes, manners, and morals. It set forth a simple determinist sequence. Scientific discoveries and inventions instigate changes first in the economic organization and social habits that are most closely associated with them; thus factories and cities, corporations, and labor organizations have grown up in response to technological developments.

The next step of changes occurs in organizations one step further removed, namely, in institutions such as the family, the government, the schools, and the churches. Somewhat

93

later, as a rule, some changes occur in social philosophies and codes of behavior.

This, of course, is no more than Marx and Engels set forth eighty-four years earlier in the Manifesto of the Communist Party. Addressing the bourgeoisie, they declared, "Your very ideas are but the outgrowth of conditions of your bourgeois production and bourgeois property, just as your jurisprudence is but the will of your class made into law for all, a will whose essential character and direction are determined by the economical conditions of existence of your class."

Recent Social Trends had no doubts about the institutional impact of technology. "Of the great social organizations," the Committee wrote, "two, the economic and governmental, are growing at a rapid rate while two others, the church and the family, have declined."

Marx and Engels would not have been distressed by this trend and could fairly claim to have foreseen it. The Manifesto speaks of "bourgeois claptrap about the family, as an institution based wholly on capital, on private gain." It noted the practical absence of the family among the proletarians and presumably looked to the family's general decline, along with bourgeois decline, which the Great Depression surely adumbrated. And yet there is a profound difference between the two documents: the Manifesto looks to technology to bring about a wholesale transformation of the society in a very short order; *Recent Social Trends* has no such apocalyptic or chiliastic view. It assumed that what had been happening would go on happening. If it was in this respect un-Hegelian, it was nonetheless far more scientific. Compared with Wesley C. Mitchell and Charles Meriam, Marx and Engels come off as rather gifted eccentrics; one could as well imagine them in white robes sitting on top of a Middlewestern hilltop with the folk of the 1840s, waiting for the end of the world. Mitchell and Meriam's world went on, and so did the trends they forecast.

Years later, President Eisenhower's Commission on National Goals met to consider the subject further. It was hardly a less distinguished group, broader in its composition and even more so perhaps in its resources. The times, of course, were different. War had come and gone; prosperity had returned; the habit, the condition of command had come to American life. President Eisenhower appointed to his Commission men who had led the great armies, governed conquered nations, launched vast scientific enterprises. Much of this is reflected in the Commission's report. It prescribed where its predecessor at most predicted. "We were not commissioned," the earlier Committee had written, "to lead the people into some new land of promise, but rather to retrace our recent wanderings."

Not so this new body of university presidents, board chairmen, former ambassadors, and generals. They had been commissioned to set forth goals and they did so, although not without awareness that there was a certain preemptive quality to the enterprise. Just what people wanted and what they understood of what they wanted was not always clear. But the report was everywhere rational, decent, optimistic, and implemental. In almost every area of concern, it was judged that more of what then was would get us where we wished to be. Thus, after the individual, concern for equality was foremost of the social questions examined. The Commission found vestiges of religious prejudice, handicaps to women, and most important, discrimination on the basis of race. It condemned them and proposed that the 1960s be the decade in which we sharply lower these last stubborn barriers.

Yet it insisted on the reality of progress. "We have more closely approached a classless society; there has been a revolution in the status of women; education is more nearly available to all; most citizens have opportunities which a century ago were dreamed by only a handful."

With equal assertiveness, it set forth a program of essentially governmental actions that could be carried forward in the

1960s, given the rates of economic growth also proposed, and that would (such everywhere was the implication or the assertion) bring about palpable and perceived further progress. Good things were ahead for the democratic process, for the quality of American culture, for meeting human needs, for the United States' role in the world. There would be a great age of science. Decades earlier, the Committee on Recent Social Trends had cautioned, "There are important elements in human life not easily stated in terms of efficiency, mechanization, institutions, rates of change.

"Happiness," the Committee noted, "is one of our most cherished goals, yet little studied by science."

Prudent observations, as the 1960s were to reveal. For in the course of that decade, one after another of the goals set forth by the Eisenhower Commission was reached and surpassed, yet in the end there was the utmost questioning among those elements of the nation concerned with such matters. Whatever the nation was by 1970, it was not happy. Forecasts had come true, goals had been met, there had been abundant success, and yet the quality of life seemed sadly deficient.

If science knew little of the sources of happiness and unhappiness, some advances have been made in measuring it, and recurrently such measures showed decline. A survey taken in 1971 found Americans quite content with their personal lives, with a sense of their own situation having improved and the expectation that it would continue to do so; but the nation was seen as having declined — the rarest phenomenon. On only one other occasion, in the Philippines in 1959, had citizens reported their nation as having declined in this way. Americans expected things to pick up for the country, but slowly. It would take time just to get back to where we had been.

Three instances will illustrate the extent to which the goals of the Eisenhower Commission were achieved during the decade for which they were set.

The economic advisers to the Commission projected an annual growth rate of the gross national product of 3.3 percent. That's what they saw happening; they suggested ways this could be increased to 4 percent and clearly hoped it would be. It was — 4 percent was precisely the growth rate for the decade.

The Commission was concerned by the inadequacy of federal government salaries and the presumed difficulty this caused in obtaining more public servants equal in competence and imagination to those in private business and professions. It called for a drastic increase in their compensation. Under President Kennedy, the principle of comparability was adopted for federal pay scales, such that executive salaries indeed rose sharply. By 1970, federal civilian employees were receiving pay raises 41 percent higher than those in private industry.

By 1960, completing high school and going to college had become the measure of achievement. The Commission noted, "In a few states, 4/5 of the youth complete four years of high school, and 1/2 enroll in an institution of higher education. This is a majestic accomplishment."

But these were all practical men; they called for a lesser goal for the nation as a whole. Within a decade they hoped at least two thirds of the youth in every state would complete twelve years of schooling, and at least one third would enter college. Yet by 1972, 56 percent of female high school graduates entered postsecondary education, and 58 percent of the males. The Commission proposed that government expenses at all levels must amount to $33 billion for education by 1970. Actually the 1970 amount was $57 billion.

Yet we were not happy. Economic growth came to be seen by many as more of a problem than a solution to our problems. The very efficiency of government managers, such as it was, came to be seen by equally many as a primary threat to things of far greater value than efficiency. Even where values stay steadily in place and few perceptions change, the 1960s did exceptional damage to the notion that government knows how to obtain the social results it nominally desires.

Education, a near universal public service, and to most minds perhaps the most important one, was hardest hit of all and will serve to illustrate this unanticipated consequence. Put plainly, in the first half of the 1960s, all manner of inquiries were launched to demonstrate what everyone knew: in education there is a reasonable and direct relation between expenditure and results. By the end of the decade, this belief was in ruins. Indeed, as expenditure increased, it appeared that results were actually declining. If there was no cause for actual alarm, it is nonetheless the case that this came to what had to be explained as the "decade that went awry."

It would be an exaggeration to depict the proposals of the Eisenhower Commission as having been uniformly achieved in the decade that followed. Unemployment levels, for example, were below 4 percent, as the Commission proposed, for only four years of the decade; but in the main the style of American national life in the ensuing period did very much reflect the concepts embodied in the Commission report, and in no one thing more than in the ideal of strong presidential leadership. This was not explicit in the report; the phrase is from an accompanying paper, but it was a precondition or almost that of the great bulk of the Commission's proposals, which envisioned a strong, confident, and purposeful United States setting things right at home and, to no small degree, abroad.

In this Bicentennial year, it is difficult for any of us (and nigh to impossible for those who are young) to realize just how total was the support of major American institutions for the policies, especially the foreign policies, of the early 1960s, which later came to be anathematized in terms that would seemingly preclude any possibility of previous endorsement. An editorial in the *New York Times* of November 3, 1963, three weeks before the assassination of President Kennedy, does, however, somewhat evoke that period. The previous day, the President of South Vietnam and his brother had been murdered in a coup. This, the chief political correspondent of the *Times* observed, "opened up a new and more hopeful phase of the war."

The *Times* editorial was emphatic to the point of being euphoric. "The coup in Saigon was inevitable, and given the stubborn refusal of President Diem to institute political reforms that had long been urged upon him, it was by this time highly desirable."

This verily was a tract for the times. In the manner of the graffito that warns, "Support mental health or I'll kill you," the liberal and reliable institutions of the United States in 1963 were quite comfortable with the view that leaders who did not carry out reforms had to be shot in the head. Leaving aside the question of murder, the faith in reform as it was then described, reform often defined as simple-minded preachiness, seems antique indeed. The 1960s saw such efforts at every level of government and after a point there was scarcely one segment of the society or another, and on occasion virtually every segment, which had come to see them as calamitous.

In defense of social science, it may be asserted that by the time these calamities had come to pass (and a good many of them were scarcely as calamitous as they may have first appeared), a good many of them had been predicted. In domestic matters in particular, the 1960s saw a burst of creative analysis that transformed our understanding of the expected consequences of a vast range of government interventions. No unified theory emerged, indeed nothing spectacularly scientific occurred at all, rather the event — it was almost that compact — had about it the quality of a religious reformation. Established institutions had become overlarge and underproductive. The suspicion spread that the needs of the institutions themselves had acquired too great a salience in the

99

scheme of things. Besides, its agents were going about selling indulgences when it could be shown that crime will be punished, that money cannot buy back innocence, nor yet can salvation be had by words.

Hence, how very different the tone of the 1970 report, *Toward Balanced Growth: Quantity with Quality,* the work of the National Goals Research Staff established in the White House by President Nixon in 1969.

In keeping with the feeling of the time that social accounting ought to be a continuous process (in the final hours of the Johnson administration, a prototype social report had been issued), the Goals staff was directed to issue an annual publication. As a matter of deliberate choice, the Hoover rather than the Eisenhower example was to be followed. This annual report was not to be a prescriptive exercise; rather its task was merely to set forth some of the key choices open to us as a nation and to examine the consequence of these choices. For the grand undertakings of yore, the counselor's statement introducing the 1970 report was perhaps not inappropriately cautionary. "A law of proportionality," this passage said, "obtains in the affairs of men. He who would make no little plans must expect to make no small mistakes."

Yet clearly there were choices to be made. The State of the Union address had forecast a $500 billion increase in gross national product in the decade then commencing, an increase greater than the whole of the growth of the American economy from 1790 to 1950. The 1970 report chose to concentrate on four emerging debates, which manifestly reflect views of considerable ambivalence about this prospective growth. These were the issues of population, of environment, of basic natural science, and of consumerism. Whatever else, such a list suggests, and clearly enough, that quality of life, whatever exactly it might be, was becoming an almost political issue in a way that had never occurred before.

In 1971, the Institute for Social Research of the University of

Michigan conducted a survey of the subject, the first of its kind. The results sufficiently confirmed the judgment of the national Goals Research Staff that emerging debates about American goals were of a different order from those current at midcentury. By contrast with the more established categories of national goals, where all could agree that conditions improved and most could desire that they go on doing so, the predominant judgment about the quality of life was that it had deteriorated. If the Committee on Recent Social Trends had maintained its psychological buoyancy in the face of economic collapse, the American public four decades later seemed in almost the opposite circumstance. Half the sample felt that on balance life had not changed, or that where change had occurred, the good had about evened out the bad. But of the remaining half, two out of three felt that, all things considered, things were getting worse.

There were some bitter Americans, hating the life America gave them. Nine percent of those interviewed said they would like to settle for good in some other country. Another 6 percent could imagine doing so. These sentiments would not disturb other nations; at least it would come as no surprise to them. In Europe, for example, even the most stable and outwardly successful societies win only moderate approval from their citizens, of whom considerable numbers not only continue to talk of emigrating, but do emigrate; nor should it be assumed that the findings disturbed Americans in the sense of surprising them. Little is revealed which in some manner we had not been telling one another for some time. An announcement of the survey findings was perhaps slightly oblique. Some groups are far more critical of the quality of American life than others. Surprisingly, persons most satisfied generally with life in the United States today are those who have ostensibly gained the least, those with the smallest incomes and the least education. This was not exclusively so in that study as in others. Black Americans are shown to be substantially less satisfied with their lives than whites, but this accords with the common-sense judgment that persons who have been discriminated against and who are less well off by many, if not most, indicators of economic well-being, will reflect this disadvantage in their psychological attitudes. But why should those better off feel worse off?

Before adopting too simple a view of this anomaly, which is to say before assuming that the middle class is somehow rising in revolt against fraudulent values and false consciousness, it is well to recall James Q. Wilson's dictum that in a liberal society, almost all political arguments are arguments within the middle class. The Communist Manifesto was an argument within the European bourgeoisie. A clue to the nature of the argument can be had from Angus Campbell's comment on the responses to that sample of Americans who were interviewed on the quality of life. "Most prominent of their criticisms is the belief that economic conditions have worsened, with inflation and taxation most frequently mentioned."

Crime, drug use, declining morality, public protests and disorders, and various aspects of environmental pollution are seen by significant numbers of people as evidence of things getting worse. An image of W. E. B. Du Bois helps clarify these responses. He once compared a people to a vast army on the march, spread out for miles; those in the van know little of events in the rear and vice versa; those in the middle get only confused reports from either end; complete misunderstanding and total ignorance are equally common. And yet one event is in process: the group is on the move.

Heading where? One persuasive hypothesis is that in the first half of this century the American system turned from laissez faire to rationalization and an increasingly managerial government. The world view entrenched before World War II is now under attack and an alternative scheme that cherishes pluralism, affiliations with local communities, and fulfillment rather than perfection is taking shape. We acquire some sense of this movement from the three presidential reports that have been discussed. The first, arising — to public affairs and to society at large — of just that rationality, system, and management which, in economic activity and business, had showed both extraordinary potential and performance. The second report was all rationality and systematic management, as the first report would have wished. The third report, however, reflected the disillusion and anxiety that all this system and management had somehow brought about. These were not then disconnected events; the one flowed from the other.

In just this sense, it is essential that the unhappy citizens, whose reponses Angus Campbell and others describe, not be seen as a uniform group reflecting a common opinion. To the absolute contrary, it should be assumed that what we see here is an amalgam of unhappiness, three reasonably distinct groups expressing unhappiness from three reasonably distinct perspectives: that of the old, and now clearly recessive, laissez-faire America and that of the emergent, affective post-industrial America. This latter group includes many whose concerns are as much religious in nature as secular — persons for whom materialism, be it individualistic or collective, is simply not a sufficient view of human nature.

In considering critical choices that Americans face with respect to the quality of life in the society, the first choice has got to do with whether the discussion will go forth with a reasonable respect for the ascertainable facts and a sufficient tolerance of the unavoidable complexity, such as the different sources of unhappiness I have described. We are not unhappy about the same things. In goodly measure, what we are unhappy about is one another. Nothing will come of merely extrapolating the class-bound and generational-bound discontents of any one group into a generalized assertion. Happily, if unavoidably, the great simplifiers are much in evidence, although possibly not so much as in some distant past. There are, to use David Riesman's phrase, "great complexifiers abroad in the land" also.

Let us join forces with the latter, and in that spirit offer a simple test.

In a general way, is it not the case that concern for the quality of life, that term, is seen as an advanced view, and not unreasonably associated with a progressive political position? And is it not equally the case that a report that twice as many Americans feel the quality of life is deteriorating as find it improving has about it a certain penumbral suggestion of progressiveness? And yet examine more closely the specifics that the Michigan survey tells us were complained about: inflation, taxation, crime, drug use, declining morality, public protest, disorders, environmental pollution. Only the last item, environmental pollution, is a matter that would appear in a wide spectrum of contemporary opinion. Other than that, the complainants present themselves as anything but progressive in their views. Far from desiring change, it is the fact of *change* that evidently persuades them that the quality of life has deteriorated. Wherefore, on pain of seeing concern for the quality of life as a positively regressive force in contemporary public affairs, it seems prudent to accept that it is in fact a complex one, mingling with various and often contrary views of which those thought to be the most progressive are scarcely the most evident.

What seems reasonable is to suppose that this amalgam of complainants is made up of persons who can be found in almost every point on Du Bois' line of march. There will be those for whom change has been unwelcome, those for whom change has been disappointing, and those for whom change has not come fast enough. There is no escaping this complexity; a statement of choices has to respond to the concerns of each of these tendencies in American opinion.

And so to conclude, in 1971 a judgment on the nature of

complaints about the quality of life in the United States might have concluded with that caveat, that at least a sizable, and possibly predominant, element among those dissatisfied were reflecting essentially conservative social views. Such persons were attached to old American standards, were troubled by new standards and new manners. This fits with the pattern in which individuals found themselves well enough off but thought the nation in terrible shape. But this conservative group had at least the advantage of thinking the old values were right and did work, and with the onset of the 1970s had the psychological reward of a national administration much given to reassuring them on that point.

Then came Watergate, a disgrace without equivalent in American history. There is no satisfactory way to judge just how permanent will be the effect of singular events, nor yet always to know which indeed are singular. First the 1960s saw a President who had promised peace wage war. Surveys conducted in 1971 and 1972 showed the damage of these and other traumas. "The people's assessment of the state of the nation in 1970," they write, "was unquestionably the most pessimistic recorded since the introduction of public opinion polling in the midst of the Great Depression."

And then in the 1970s came the shock of a President who had promised probity revealed as having succumbed to sickening dismay and corruption.

These may indeed be idiosyncratic events. Adam Smith's dictum of 200 years ago, that "there is a deal of ruin in the nation," may yet prove the greater wisdom. The evidence seems to be that there is or has been a cyclical movement of confidence from peaks to troughs. The 1950s was surely a peak, as the report of President Eisenhower's Commission would suggest; just as surely the 1970s and the Nixon study suggest a trough. American leaders have fallen from grace before and, in truth, we have lost wars before. It is at least possible, and probable, that we commence to measure levels of public con-

fidence at a peak moment such that things now look more ominous than they will once a full cycle has been recorded. On
the other hand, it is possible that measurement will affect the
observation and reinforce the decline. Patterns of war abroad,
the subordination of laws and liberties at home may indeed
prove the pattern of a civilization changing its character. Either way, and surely it will take a generation before anyone
could reasonably contend that there was sufficient evidence to
judge, in the near term we must assume that every element of
American opinion has been hard hit and that none approaches
the third century with overgreat confidence. Old standards
have been betrayed, new standards have not been accepted,
the ameliorists and the managers in the middle can't seem to
deliver.

It must be emphasized that the declining trust in government, a key element surely in assessing the quality of life,
commenced well before Watergate. It commenced with the assassination of President Kennedy and has declined with successive shocks to confidence ever since. But there is no longer
much room for further decline. In truth, the case could be
made in Marxist-Leninist terms that the United States is in a
prerevolutionary condition, especially so in the added context
of unemployment, economic stagnation, and failure in a
foreign war which, if not waged for imperialist purposes, was
surely waged in a quintessentially imperialist setting. And
yet there would be virtually no way to judge which direction a
genuine upheaval might take, save to speculate that it would
not, in the first instance, be radical. We dismiss the Marxist-
Leninist hypothesis. The doctrine has been wrong about almost everything else. Why should it be right about the
United States? We assume there is a deal of ruin in a nation,
and we note how little damage has been done in substantive
terms. We do not, however, assume that there will be a cyclical return to the buoyancy of, say, the 1950s.

There are choices to be made which lead in different combinations to quite different outcomes and some of these are likely to be anything but buoyant. There are, in any event, deep-set trends in the society that lead us away from the conditions of the past. These need to be worked out, for it is here that the critical choices of the third century must be made.

Questions and Answers

Since Ambassador Moynihan was engaged that evening, the usual discussion at the Parkman House was traded off for an extended question and answer period immediately after his address. The questions handed up from the floor were numerous, and were fairly evenly divided among three topics, the future of capitalism, the future of the United Nations, and Mr. Moynihan's immediate political plans. On the first two he spoke at length; on the third, very briefly, and then only at the end of the session.

It went thus:

Q. Given the socialistic tendencies of the Western democracies, does capitalism have a chance of survival in the United States, or are we going the route of Great Britain?

A. Well, it depends on whether you teach at Harvard or M.I.T. If you send your children to M.I.T., we'll do all right. I think one of the issues of the coming decade and generation is how much government we want in this society. We have reached the point where it represents about 35 percent of the gross national product, and that does seem to be a critical mass. If you get much beyond 35 percent things get so bad that government spends more and more of its time making up for the mistakes it has already made. I would like to see us hold about where we are. Actually this is a very large question, and I don't see how any answer to it could be substantiated statistically. As for socialism, in the Western democracies, nothing astounds me more than the statements typically made about, for example, the government of West Germany. It is always being referred to as "hard-headed, capitalist, conservative." Actually it is a socialist government too, but one which produces a lot of goods and services and wishes to go on doing so.

Q. What programs do you propose in order to establish a higher standard of living, and to allow the less fortunate to take advantage of the opportunities available to the wealthy?

A. Answering that question is a superhuman task. I honestly don't know what ought to be done. I think there are psychological studies on present- and future-orientedness. I think they show a convergence of views of persons in what are called the lower and the upper classes. It is those in between who of necessity talk and think most about the future. I am no more complex than the next fellow on things I am enthusiastic about, and I have thought for some years that we ought to establish a guaranteed income in this country. We almost did it in the Family Assistance Plan. It passed the House of Representatives twice. It was a kind of welfare reform, but beyond that it was an income guarantee such that society could decently say it was providing a minimum for everyone and did not have to go on providing everything else as well. It almost passed, and I said in 1970 that if it did not pass then it probably would not pass in this decade. But we can still hope.

Q. Do you think it is in the best interest of the United States to use food as an economic weapon?

A. Clearly you don't use food as a weapon against people who are starving. But with nations that are well enough fed but would like to eat more steak and less macaroni, it is reasonable to negotiate for things you reasonably want, like fewer backfire bombers. Food is one of the things we can offer to people, not just as a positive commodity, such as grain, but as an example of what it is to be a society in which reasonably independent producers grow food well. Communists can't grow food, and it's a failure they can't quite explain. We can, and the world should know why.

Q. Some economists have predicted that coalitions of re-source-rich African and Latin American countries will attempt to drive up the prices of minerals and raw materials much as the Arabs have done with oil. What can be done to keep this from happening?

A. I think that now, with the events of 1973 falling into perspective, we are coming to see that oil is unique. Arab oil is produced in a small number of countries, many of which do not so urgently need the revenue they get from it as to hold it back from the market. At the same time it is unique in that it is a commodity other nations absolutely must have. I say to you that there is no prospect of any equivalent monopoly being formed with anything remotely like the same conse-quences. It has taken some of the developing nations a while to realize this, but they are now realizing it. While we had a stormy session in the Thirtieth General Assembly of the United Nations, it was preceded by the Seventh Special Ses-sion, which was devoted to issues of development involving the industrial and the nonindustrial worlds. Two things came out: what the most industrial country in the world, the United States, sells mostly abroad is food, and nations that thought of themselves as producers of raw materials, like India, mostly import raw materials.

After a two-year sequence in which one after another of these conferences met and deadlocked, we were spitting mad, with deepening discord and division. But we ended with unanimous agreement. Then last week at the meeting of the General Council of the United Nations Development Program, I gave a little report on what we had done in the five months since the end of the Special Session. And I could already point to a $5 billion annual increase in the transfer of resources to developing countries, just coming out of that agreement.

The specific problem is that those oil prices, while inconvenient to us, and costly to some other developed nations, were disastrous to the really poor countries. The poorest of the poor, and just the poor generally, have been terribly hurt by the quadrupling of oil prices, and the world has not yet found a solution to this problem. But let it be clear that it was not the Western industrial nations that did that, and let me say that point is sinking in. You mustn't expect too much of people. It takes a couple of years to notice things like that, to find a language in which to say, "My brother, you did this to me." But that language is emerging, and none too soon. The view that some of the developing countries are blocked in hostility toward the United States and Western Europe is less and less a true reflection of the facts. On the contrary, they recognize that the only prospect they have is through a fruitful economic relation with us, and this shows in day-to-day behavior in a place like the U.N.

Q. On the basis of your experience with the United Nations, what changes in its organization do you think should be made to make it more effective?

A. In answering that question I'd like to distinguish between aspects of the United Nations. The General Assembly connotes one set of phenomena; the Security Council, a very different set. I once said to a Chicago journalist that the Security Council is to the General Assembly as the Chicago City Council is to an international convention of World Federalists. Matters of quite different seriousness and substance take place in the two bodies. In the General Assembly the most significant change one could hope for is continued American insistence on a single standard of behavior among the countries of the world, particularly on the issue of human rights, which is known to be not only our particular national issue, but that of the democracies as a group. If the language of human rights is to go on being used in the General Assembly, then the facts of human rights have to be expressed. What I would hope to see is the emergence of a parliamentary caucus in the General Assembly in which the two dozen or so democracies left in the world would work together on issues that specifically concern liberal and illiberal societies.

In the Security Council, in the main, the issue is not procedure, it is the willingness of governments to see that things are dealt with. That is not the kind of thing that changes as a consequence of organizational reform. In the great specialized agencies of the United Nations, some of which do fair work, the problem is that of vastly compounding the rewards for government service. Those jobs are precious; anybody who gets one gets it for life.

Q. The results of our foreign policy in the past ten years have been at best mediocre. Don't you think it is time the United States established a career-oriented diplomatic corps and ended the practice of appointing political cronies and campaign contributors as ambassadors?

A. I have spent the last ten months pulling arrows out of my back that were planted there by people who have acquired their skills through long professional practice, as a consequence of tenure. I can deal with amateurs, who have no more experience in this business than myself. It's the pros that give me problems.

About two thirds of our ambassadors are career diplomats. We have a good foreign service. Like any institution, it is in no way diminished by the infusion of people who come in (mostly at the top level, unfortunately) with different views, reflecting the changing political climate. I have seen many of the battles that take place — normally between noncareer and career people on both sides. There are few issues on which they separate. As to the "purchase" of ambassadorships, I know I am supposed to be against it, but I keep thinking of Lord Melbourne's wonderful remark that the Order of the Garter was his favorite "because there was no damn nonsense about merit."

Q. Ronald Reagan has said that the United Nations is on its last legs. Do you see a decrease in U.S. involvement in the U.N.? If so, do you approve? And with your permission, Ambassador, I'll combine that with a second question. What can you tell us about why you resigned as ambassador to the United Nations?

A. I wish to speak respectfully of the former governor of California. That great leader of the Republican Party, Senator Everett Dirksen of Illinois, was once required to speak in the Senate on behalf of an Illinoisan who had been nominated for a post by President Eisenhower, when party loyalty required him to speak despite inclinations otherwise. He told his fellow senators, "Gentlemen, I rise to tell you that I hold this nominee in minimal high regard."

The United Nations is not on its last legs. There are people who are short-winded enough to be out of patience with it, but that's of no consequence. It's there, we're in it, and we'll stay in it. I think one of the remarkable impressions I've had of the last eight months is that while I've heard from a great many people who have been annoyed with things that have happened at the U.N., I don't think I've gotten ten letters out of what is now 50,000 that I've tried to answer that say, "Get out of that place." The question is, rather, how to behave while you're in. It's natural enough to be annoyed from time to time with what happens there. But you don't get rid of the Assembly because you don't happen to like the particular day's proceedings.

Then with a brisk grin: You asked a second question, Mr. Chairman, but I've forgotten what that second question was.

Q. Then let me ask you just one more, Mr. Ambassador. We promised that we would not ask you about your future political plans, but in reading through the many questions that have been submitted, we feel that the next question becomes unavoidable. What *are* your political plans?

A. I have none. Thank you.

6

The American Bicentennial in Black and White

Vernon E. Jordan, Jr.

The penultimate speaker at the Bicentennial Forums, Vernon Jordan, appeared in Faneuil Hall on April 6, 1976 — the day after a black attorney had been attacked without provocation and beaten with the pole of an American flag by two white teen-age boys in Boston's City Hall Plaza. To protest this pointless act of violence, Jordan began with a powerful denunciation not only of this attack but of the health of a city and a culture in which it could take place. He was warmly received by an audience one-third black and two-thirds white, and the applause he received came equally from both.

Executive director of the National Urban League since 1972, Dr. Jordan has served with the NAACP as field director in Georgia, with the U.S. Office of Economic Opportunity, and as Director of the Southern Regional Council's Voter Education Project. He has held other government posts and has been a director of numerous organizations both in business and in public affairs.

Dr. Jordan holds a B.A. degree from DePauw University, a J.D. degree from Howard University Law School, and honorary degrees from seventeen colleges and universities. He has written extensively for major publications, and his current newspaper column, "To Be Equal," appears in 120 newspapers.

A Bicentennial year is most often associated with celebrations and with reflections on the past. America's Bicentennial, however, cannot afford such a self-indulgent luxury. America's Bicentennial cannot afford to be content with a celebration of a past whose consequences have yet to be sorted out and whose legacy is clouded by an uncertain future.

It is, however, a time for seeking within the past the ideals and principles that may help us deal with the awesome problems we face as a nation today. That search need go no further than the still-to-be-fulfilled promise embodied in our Declaration of Independence: ". . . that all Men are created equal, that they are endowed by their Creator with certain unalienable rights, that among these are Life, Liberty, and the Pursuit of Happiness."

It was those words and the promise they held forth that won America's independence, not the valiant and bitter military struggle alone. John Adams derided the idea that the Revolution was won on battlefields when he said, "The revolution was won in men's minds." And the core of that revolution of the mind was the promise of equality and the concept of democracy.

The gap between the promise of the Declaration and the reality of America's imperfect democracy is especially seen in the conditions afflicting black people and other minorities. For a strong thread of hypocrisy runs through America's history, from the time a slaveowner, Thomas Jefferson, penned the immortal words of the Declaration, to our own time when the constitutional rights of little black children are denied by unruly mobs.

Thus, some black citizens see the Bicentennial as an event that is not relevant to them — as a celebration from which the events of the past and present only serve as reminders of oppression and bitterness. Rejected by America's policies through the ages, some black people now reject the birthday party to which they have been reluctantly invited.

I do not share that view. If I did, I would not be here today. To me, the Bicentennial represents an opportunity to remind a forgetting nation of the ideals that inspired its birth and of the fact that this nation's future depends to a large extent upon its ability to reconcile those ideals to its public policy. We can enthusiastically support the principles of equality, while at the same time point to the persistent violation of those principles.

Those Americans who claim to believe in democracy and in democratic ideals must pay heed to our just cause and to our reminders that the barriers of race, of poverty, and of joblessness should not be tolerated in the birthplace of liberty and the fount of equality. America's birthday celebration is tarnished because it occurs in a year of intolerably high unemployment, of rising poverty, and of continued national economic recession. Thus, our Bicentennial must be the occasion, not merely for self-congratulation, but for a critical appraisal of what must be done to extend our national ideals to all of our citizens. The grim reality of unequal opportunity for many millions of Americans should inspire us to positive actions to reorder our national priorities and to fulfill the aspirations of all of our people.

There are today in America over 24 million people officially classified as poor. Some estimates place the number at 40 million, because the official poverty line has lagged behind rising prices. There are today, in America, over 7 million people officially classified as unemployed, and, if we add to them 5 million discouraged workers who have given up looking for nonexistent jobs, and over 3 million part-time workers who want full-time work, we find some 15 million people unemployed or subemployed. And that does not even include about 2 million people who work full-time for below poverty level wages.

The largest share of this burden has been borne by black people; a fourth of the black work force is unemployed. Up to two thirds of black teen-agers are jobless. A third of all black families are poor, and half of them don't get a single penny from welfare. And black family income is slipping only to a little more than half the white family income. Indeed, in almost every measure of socioeconomic status, blacks lag behind whites, and in many instances the gap is growing, not closing.

Despite the current popularity of optimistic predictions about the economy, it is clear that unemployment and poverty will continue to remain at unconscionably high levels. Administration spokesmen predict unemployment will still be at the 7 million level by year's end, and full employment is now universally regarded as unattainable.

To accept this, however, is to accept continued joblessness for many millions of people who desperately want to work — black and white alike. To accept this is to doom those people and their children to marginal economic existence and to rob America of the full prosperity for all that it is capable of achieving. And to accept this is to doom ourselves to artificially lowered living standards and federal budget deficits.

For every million people out of work, the government loses $16 billion in lost tax receipts and unemployment benefits. This year alone, abnormally high unemployment rates cost our economy over $150 billion in lost economic growth. This year alone, the federal government will spend over $40 billion in unemployment compensation and welfare costs, most of which would not be necessary if we had full employment.

If our nation had implemented a full employment policy twenty years ago, we would have produced in that time an extra $2 trillion worth of goods and services, and federal tax receipts would have gained some $500 billion. Thus, we must ask whether we can afford *not* to have full employment.

All of this is reminiscent of Whitney Young's proposal for a Domestic Marshall Plan, made almost fifteen years ago. Had Young's plan been accepted, we would today have erased the discrimination that oppresses black people, put our economy on a full employment and full productivity basis, and rescued our urban areas from the deterioration that threatens their existence.

Indeed, it is a tribute to Young's stature and his vision to realize that his plan is not dated today. Rather, it is more relevant than ever to marshal our public and private resources, to reverse the downward spiral of our society's well-being.

In adapting Whitney Young's Marshall Plan to the 1970s, we should consider two basic, new proposals that would end the joblessness and dependency. First, our nation desperately needs a national full employment policy that guarantees a decent job at a decent wage to all Americans able to work. I envision a three-pronged effort to achieve a national full employment policy, including, first, incentives to private industry to recruit, train, and hire the jobless. The private sector can't do the job alone, but public policies that make it less attractive for business to hire more workers compound the difficulty. Federal regulations, subsidies, and tax incentives should all be directed at increasing the private sector's ability to create jobs.

The second step would be for the federal government to create a public works program along the lines of the old WPA (Works Progress Administration) that helped sustain millions during the Depression of the 1930s. Those public works projects lined our country with roads, bridges, schoolhouses, and other public facilities still in use today. A similar program in the 1970s would not only create jobs, but would provide a new generation of vitally needed houses, transportation facilities, and other public works our nation needs.

And third, a vastly expanded public service employment program that would help fill the pressing need for public services while assuring employment opportunities for millions of people. In the Johnson administration a presidential commission determined that public sector manpower needs in conservation, safety, education, and health could accommodate some 5 million new jobs, offering an opportunity to sharply improve necessary public services. A national full employment policy, along the lines I have outlined here, would make unemployment a thing of the past, turn revenue consumers into revenue producers, generate tax income to pay for itself, and remove the curse of joblessness from the land.

There would still be, however, people unable to work — people in need of assistance to maintain the basic necessities of a decent life. The welfare system is supposed to do this, but I cannot imagine a system more destructive of human initiative and self-respect, a system more wasteful in its administrative procedures, a system more inconsistent in the gap between its stated goals and its actual practice than our present welfare system.

But its worst fault is that it does not work. The welfare system for the poor is not nearly as efficient as the welfare system of tax loopholes and subsidies for the wealthy. That's why there is growing support for a welfare reform program that assures a livable, minimum income, while relieving state and local governments of the increasing burden of providing for the needs of the poor.

I believe, and we in the Urban League believe, that the most efficient reform would be a universal refundable credit income tax that would extend a basic annual grant or tax credit to everybody. That grant would be taxable income, so that the poor would keep all of it, the near poor would keep some of it, and middle and upper income families would return it all in taxes. This system would be financed by removal of today's tax reductions and loopholes, and by the imposition of a flat tax rate on all income. Such a system would limit subsidies to those in need, and not, as at present, to the better off. It would supplement the income of working families who cannot make ends meet. Because the tax credit would be automatic and universal, it would bring big savings in administrative costs, and reduce abuses so prevalent in the present system.

My proposals for a national full employment policy and for a universal refundable credit income tax are pro-work, pro-human dignity proposals. They would increase national productivity, stimulate the economy, end unemployment and lessen poverty, and would go a long way toward removing the economic causes of racial antagonism.

It is too often forgotten in America, too often forgotten by our political leadership, that more white people than black people are out of work, that more white people than black people in America are poor, and that there are more white people receiving welfare in America than there are black people receiving welfare in America; and it is too often forgotten that while black people suffer disproportionately higher rates of economic hardship, five times as many whites are jobless, and twice as many whites than blacks are poor.

So these issues cannot be framed in racial terms; they cannot be seen solely as "black" issues. Just as more white people than black people benefited from the social programs of the 1960s, so, too, would more white people than black people gain from full employment and from welfare reform.

But there is another view in America, a view that says we can't afford full employment programs, a view that says we can't afford income maintenance programs and other needed reforms. It is a view that argues that the federal government has become too big, and that it should retreat from social and economic intervention in our society. This view, which I term "the new minimalism," counsels planned withdrawal from national greatness that is subversive of ideas of equality embedded in the Declaration of Independence. And the new minimalism is wrong in its facts.

For the fact is that the federal share in the economy has not risen at all. Between 1953 and 1973 the federal budget has held steady at about 20 percent of the gross national product. The slight rise since 1973 is directly attributable to recession-related costs of unemployment compensation and welfare. That federal debt that's supposed to be so high is only about 26 percent of the gross national product. Back in 1950 the federal debt was an astonishing 82 percent of the gross national product.

Obviously, the federal government can be more responsive to the needs of its citizens and the private sector. The federal government can be more efficient and more productive. The federal government needs to take a hard-nosed look at costs, and keep them to the minimum necessary, but it also must take a hard-nosed look at national needs, and supply them to the maximum extent necessary. And I am convinced that just fussing at bureaucrats and just fussing at Washington won't put people to work, nor will it take us out of the cycle of boom and bust that retards our progress.

It is a measure of the political crisis our nation is in today that so many of the candidates for the presidency, including the incumbent President himself, are running campaigns *against* the government that they say they want to lead, and are running *against* federal activism. If we examine the content of the attacks on the federal government, we are forced to the conclusion that they constitute a blueprint for national disaster.

Less government means less protection for people without resources. Less spending means fewer desperately needed social programs and stark hunger for those in poverty. Fewer government employees mean fewer public services, less government interference means abandonment of civil-rights enforcement.

So let's not be fooled by the siren song of federal retreat from national goals, national objectives, and national reforms. Whether it's wrapped in slogans like "the new realism," or "the new federalism," or another catchy phrase, it's the same old license to exploit poor people and keep black people down.

This Bicentennial year should be the occasion of a giant step forward, not a shameful retreat into the failed formulas of the past. It should be a year in which the nation reflects upon its often sad history, and then acts upon the lessons it learns from that history. It should be a year in which the nation finally comes to understand that black disadvantage in America is the result of special treatment for black people for over 400 years, and that now, a new, positive kind of special treatment is needed to make up for the past.

Lyndon Johnson said it so well a few weeks before he died. "To be black in a white society," he said, "is not to stand on level and equal ground. While the races may stand side by side, whites stand on history's mountain, and blacks stand in history's hollow. Until we overcome unequal history, we cannot overcome unequal opportunity."

Let us then strive to overcome the unequal history we have shared these four centuries. Let us, black and white together, come together in friendship and mutual respect; let us forge together a creative partnership that will make our nation, our region, our state the light of all mankind. Let us be mindful of our obligations to a tortured past, a difficult present, and, above all, to a brighter future.

Let us have faith in ourselves and our ability to transcend the divisions of race and class together, and to build a true democracy. Interestingly, black people have that faith, and it was that faith that helped us to survive the harsh past, and led us to become the initiator, the cutting edge, the moral force that moved America to change its ways, and to strive toward its potential for greatness. Black people, interestingly, ironically, have that faith because this is our land, too. The first American to fall before British bullets was a black runaway slave — Crispus Attucks. Five thousand black soldiers fought side by side with white soldiers in the revolutionary army that won our independence.

Yes, this is our land too. And this nation, America, its political leadership, too often forgets that this America is sprinkled with our sweat, watered with our tears, and fertilized with our blood. America too often forgets that us black folk helped to build America's power and glory, that we dug 'taters and toted cotton and lifted bales and sank the canals and laid the railroad tracks that linked ocean to ocean. Black people, too, sing "God Bless America." Black people, too, sing "O beautiful for spacious skies, for amber waves of grain." Black people, too, pledge allegiance to the flag and what it represents.

We've died in America's every war, even when we were in bondage, even when we were forced into segregated units. Our blood was shed on the fields of Valley Forge, and beaches of Normandy, the island of Iwo Jima, and in the jungles of Vietnam, where we died in disproportionate numbers.

Yes, this is our land, it is the land that we live in, it is the land that we have sacrificed for, it is the land that we still believe in. Our faith in our nation is boundless. It is faith that laments the injustices of the past and present, but knows that the sleeping giant that is America, the great nation whose beauty and whose freedoms will one day be extended to all of its children will awake from its moral slumber, and that, somehow, we shall overcome.

About three weeks ago, I had a very interesting, exciting, experience. I was invited by joint resolution of the House and the Senate of the General Assembly of South Carolina to address a joint session of the South Carolina legislature. I got to Columbia the night before, and I spent the night in the Wade Hampton Hotel. Those of you who know your American history know the place and the role of Wade Hampton in South Carolina. The morning of my speech I walked out of the Wade Hampton Hotel, across the street to the Capitol, and on my way to the Capitol steps I passed a statue of Ben "Pitchfork" Tillman. I ascended the stairs, entered the legislative reception area of the state Capitol, and saw a statue of John C. Calhoun. As I entered the Speaker's office, I saw, inscribed in the marble wall, the document of secession of the state of South Carolina from the Union.

Then a joint escort committee from the House and the Senate came to the Speaker's office and escorted me into the hall. And then in joint session, as my presence was announced, thirteen black legislators in the state of South Carolina and their white counterparts rose. At the Speaker's table were the Speaker and the clerk of the court and the lieutenant governor in robes, not white robes, robes. As I rose to make my speech, hanging over my head were three flags, the flag of the state of South Carolina, the flag of the United States of America, and the flag of Jefferson Davis. And there I made my talk, and received a marvelous response and ovation, and meeting me in the aisle to shake my hand was Senator Gressette, who after 1954 in South Carolina carried the Gressette committees all over the state to maintain segregated education. Meeting me also in the middle of the aisle was Mr. Blatt, who had been Speaker of the House of South Carolina for almost forty years, and who after the 1954 Supreme Court decision stood in the well of that assembly and said, "Not one of my grandchildren will go to school with little black children." But he greeted me and he said, "Thank you for what you had to say."

I left there and went to a luncheon given in my honor by the governor of the state of South Carolina at the Governor's Mansion. The governor made a toast, and I responded by saying, "Governor, there are two strangers in this governor's mansion, me as a black man and you as a Republican governor of the state of South Carolina."

I suggest that bit of experience to you as one who grew up in Georgia, who grew up in the South, who experienced firsthand the brutality and the meanness of a segregated society. When I called my mother to say, "Mama, I'm in South Carolina and I'm going to speak to the joint session of the legislature today," her only response was "My God!"

Which merely suggests that if the state of Wade Hampton and the state of Ben "Pitchfork" Tillman and the state of John C. Calhoun, and the state of Strom Thurmond, and the state of

James F. Byrnes can change, and a little black boy from Atlanta can stand in the well of that house and speak his mind, then I am convinced that America can change, if it will.

It should not be lost on us that in 1972 George Wallace carried Flordia, but in 1976 *George Wallace carried Boston*. And there was a time that from this great city and this great state we looked down yonder and said straighten up and fly right. And we said do right by your black brothers and act consistent with morality and constitutionality. My response to that is that the chickens have come home to roost, and it's been proven that my Southland has no geographical monopoly on racism, on poverty, or on violence. Consequently, this great state of the abolitionists must get its house in order, because if you're not careful, that same region that you told ten years ago to straighten up and fly right is going to show you the way to a peaceful, open, pluralistic, and integrated society.

I'm not going to lose my faith in the possibilities of America because I have seen it change, and I have seen it change when men and women in leadership positions cared, and acted, based upon that caring, and made something happen.

So I leave you with the words of my predecessor, Whitney Young, who said once, "I do have faith in America" — not so much in a sudden upsurge of morality, nor in a new surge toward greater patriotism — but I believe in the intrinsic intelligence of Americans. I do not believe that we forever need to be confronted by tragedy or crises in order to act.

"I believe," said Whitney Young, "that the evidence is clear. I believe that we as a people will not wait to be embarrassed or pushed into a posture of decency. I believe that America has the strength to do what is right because it is right.

"I am convinced," said Young, "that given a kind of collective wisdom and sensitivity, Americans today can be persuaded to act creatively, and imaginatively, to make democracy work.

124

"This," said Young, "is my hope. This is my dream. This is my faith."

And the question that black people in Boston and black people in America would ask of this community and of this state is, Do you share that hope? Do you share that dream, and do you share that faith? We await the answer.

Questions and Discussion

The evening discussion at the Parkman House was largely a dialogue between Vernon Jordan and a group of leading figures in Boston's black community. But it was opened by Mayor White, who alluded to the unprovoked beating of a black attorney by two white teen-agers the day before in Boston's City Hall Plaza, and then raised a complex of questions that set the tone for the entire discussion. Is Boston unique, or is it representative of other cities in the nation with a substantial black population? "I sense a diminution of interest in black problems, less liberal support of black efforts, a decrease in economic progress among blacks. And I wonder whether all this is merely a natural slowing-down process, or whether there wasn't really as much progress in the 1960s as we thought there was, or whether it bodes something ominous for the blacks in the 1970s. Second, is what we're having in Boston the bursting of the abscess, an inevitable crescendo before we can really begin to bind the wounds? Were the 1960s a bit of a mirage, and are the 1970s largely pretense? Are the liberals copping out? I'm not sure where we're heading, and I'd like to know."

Vernon Jordan responded at length. "I think, first, that at the time nobody really understood what the 1960s were all about. Most people viewed them as a time when the South was dealing with its own problems. Few saw them as a time when there were problems elsewhere. When I was working with the NAACP in Georgia in 1961 and 1962, CARE packages were coming to Mississippi from Harlem. Now there are few in Mississippi who couldn't send a CARE package *to* Harlem!

"The focus was all on the South, and everybody who came north to New York or Boston assumed that they were free. They hadn't even sensed how un-free they had been until we started seeking freedom in the South. I view the 1960s as a time of defining and conferring rights on blacks. And I view the 1970s as a time of implementing those rights and making them real. It is one thing to define the right to check into the Boston Sheraton. That happened in the 1960s. It's quite another thing to have the cash to check out. Nobody really understood that in the 1960s. It was not enough to say you can check in. You had to deal with jobs and economic security and get the fellow what he needed to check out. Now, defining and conferring rights is much easier than the enabling process that has to take place, and is taking place now in the 1970s.

"If you talk about the liberals, whether in the South or in the North, it's all right as long as you talk about what's going on over yonder. But when it comes home to them, it's a different process. I have problems with all my liberal friends these days. It started in 1968, when they told me there wasn't a dime's worth of difference between Humphrey and Nixon. Liberal friends of mine who used to come south got a great kick out of bringing CARE packages. And they get a charge out of funding the stick kids who come north from Mississippi with mud on their shoes. But if I come north to New York and go into some of their offices in my Brooks Brothers suit, they say, well, you got it made and you don't need it, so how can we get a charge out of funding you? What's needed now is more than the process of defining and conferring. What's needed

126

now is the process of enabling, and that is a very different thing. Nobody really wants to deal with it.

"Then there's another problem nobody anticipated. Nobody expected, when they first started talking about equal employment opportunity, that they were heading into a recession. Labor people take the position that affirmative action rights are not as important as seniority rights, because seniority rights have become an issue of vested interest. And that is not just a black issue, it's one that transcends race. You talk to any black union man who has twenty years' seniority, he won't talk about affirmative action, he'll talk about seniority. Because he's got it. I've talked to most of the major labor leaders who've been around for a long time, and they all talk about seniority, because they worked hard to get it. You can't talk to them about shared work, or a four-day work week, as opposed to laying off 500 people. In our relations with the Jewish community, when we talked to them about affirmative action, they didn't want to hear about quotas or goals, guidelines and timetables, because of their own historic experience with quotas.

"So in the implementation process, strains always develop in traditional alliances. That's the story of the 1970s. A strain isn't necessarily the end of something. A strain is like an argument between me and my wife. We have an argument, but we don't divorce. But I think these strains have impeded black progress in the 1970s.

"Another block to progress is that some politicians, beginning with the election of Richard Nixon, said they had tried integration and various black programs, and they hadn't worked. They did not see that the response was never commensurate with the need. And they said the reason for the recession is all those social programs we tried to run in the 1960s. They totally ignored the $200 billion we spent on the Vietnam war, the real cause of the recession. There just hasn't

127

been the kind of leadership in solving black problems since 1968 that there had been from 1960 until that year."

On the question why this failure of leadership occurred, a leading member of the black community in Boston expressed the opinion that no leader since Roosevelt — including Kennedy, Truman, and Johnson — had the administrative ability to carry out a program of the scope and complexity needed to solve the problems. A prominent black educator suggested that what was really lacking was not administrative ability so much as the will on the part of politicians, particularly in the North, to implement programs for improvement of the condition of the blacks. She could see no reason why, if the South could be made to solve these problesm in the 1960s, the North couldn't be made to do so in the 1970s.

At this point a black newsman recalled the question with which Mayor Kevin White had opened the discussion, and particularly White's point about the diminution of interest in black problems and a decline in leadership. He asked Jordan to comment on these matters.

In response to these questions Jordan made the most hopeful statement of the evening. "It is true," he began, "that in the last ten years the gap between black and white income has got measurably worse. And people constantly ask where is the black leadership that was so evident in the 1960s? For then they saw us marching and singing, in Shrevesport, Jackson, and Birmingham. They could see Martin and Whitney, Roy, and John Lewis, Randolph, and the rest. Nobody ever questioned that leadership, and they were great leaders for the era.

"But it is also possible to document some fantastic measures of progress over the last ten years, even in Boston. In the North alone, the number of blacks in college is incredibly higher than it was ten years ago. One way to measure progress is by the permeation of blacks into areas of the society from which they had previously been excluded. If you look at the black community now, there are five new leadership classes that simply did not exist ten years ago. The first of these is the elected and appointed officials. How many blacks were there in the Massachusetts legislature ten years ago? Now there are 13. The South in 1965 had 70 black elected officials in the eleven states of the open Confederacy. Now there are more than 1200. There are 100 black mayors and judges. I have a classmate who was appointed by Reubin Askew to the Supreme Court of Florida, Joe Hatchett. My old law associate, Horace Ward, now sits on the civil court of Fulton County, Georgia, appointed by Jimmy Carter. That's one leadership class, and it means that there are black people now sitting in places of public policy-making where they never sat before. All that is a direct result of the Voting Rights Act of 1965.

"A second new leadership class in the black community is all those black people who today are managing, administering, running multimillion-dollar agencies, institutions, and corporations. Ten years ago this group did not exist. Ten years ago Lovell Dyett would not have been giving the news on Channel 7. Ten years ago Paul Parks would not be running the Education Department of the state of Massachusetts. Cliff Wharton wouldn't be president of Michigan State. Now that's a whole new leadership class. It's got resources, it's got staff, and it has the ability to manage people directly as relates to issues of public policy.

"The third new leadership class is composed of blacks who have pierced the corporate veil. Ray Scruggs pioneered at AT&T in Michigan a long time ago. But he was the only one for a long time. Now I sit on four corporate boards, and every day we're hiring blacks as accountants, lawyers, planners, and in many other business capacities, and those positions give them economic security so that they can work in the Opportunities Centralization Center, the Urban League, and in community organizations in many cities and towns, so they have

129

an increasing impact on the corporate decision-making process. That's a brand-new thing: blacks on the boards of General Motors, Xerox, J. C. Penney, Federated Stores, Westinghouse.

"Now the fourth new leadership class is really important. That is the proliferation of indigenous black community leadership. If you think back to your mother and father's time, or if you think about Atlanta, or New York, or Indianapolis, or Detroit, historically all the decisions were made by 'the talented tenth.' But the Poverty Program, the Urban League Program, the Model Cities Program, all these helped to democratize black leadership. And so the local mayors no longer meet with only 'the talented tenth.'

"Finally, there are new black businesses of many, many kinds. There have long been traditional businesses in the black community: the beauty shop, the barber shop, the dry cleaner, the undertaker. Those are all our businesses. We have always buried our own. But now, to take just one field, there are not only jobs for blacks in publications, there are new publications, such as *S.S. Encore, Black Enterprise,* and *Tuesday.* Most of the white people at the meat counter who buy Parks Sausages don't know that Henry Parks is black.

"Furthermore, the black community is not monolithic, nor is it one in which decisions are handed down unilaterally. A striking example of this is the 1964 election in Arkansas, where the blacks gave 90 percent of their vote to the Democratic candidate for President and 90 percent of their vote to the Republican candidate for governor. In both these political contests race was an issue, as it always is in the black community whenever it arises. But on local issues, where race was not an issue, the blacks divided their vote according to their interests."

It was then pointed out that there seems to be organized resistance to economic advancement for blacks, and even to the threat of such advancement. The more blacks learn about the system, about getting contracts, selling, advertising, business law, and the rest, the greater the resistance becomes. The motive behind this resistance is not race but the simple fact that here is important new competition. Along with this there is an assault on black leadership, for example, the recently discovered FBI attempt to smear Martin Luther King, Jr.

To this Mayor White said that in business the whites did indeed feel the existence of the new black threat. And Vernon Jordan said he was not disturbed by this white response to effective new competition, that nobody gives up power willingly, and that he sensed some paranoia on the part of the blacks who did not want to be held accountable on the same standards as whites. He mentioned the case of an official who was accused of misusing public funds for personal travel. Some people call that charge racism, but the use of the term "racism" in this connection is to a degree paranoid. The simple fact is that a year or two after Watergate, any public official who travels privately on state money and is found out will get into the papers.

An interesting point was made by a panelist who said he had seen many cities, but that Boston had more white working poor than any other he knew. As a result, he thought, heavy work, common labor, and less attractive jobs of many kinds, which ordinarily went to blacks elsewhere, were taken by whites in Boston. "If you go down and watch the car tracks being repaired, you will find thirty men with picks and shovels, and thirty of them will be white." He felt that until the problems of Boston's white working poor could be solved or at least relieved, the blacks could not be much advanced. Mayor White was keenly interested in this observation, said he had never heard it before, and surmised that the condition could be a key factor in the Boston busing troubles.

The educator who had spoken earlier said she had hope, and with hope and perseverance the battle could be won. "I myself," she said, "in Jackson, Mississippi — a place blacks tremble just to think about — saw black and white junior high school kids playing football. Nobody could have told me I'd see that in my lifetime. If those people, from those back-woods, could be called upon to sit down and halfway behave, then I think leadership and law can be made very supportive to the white working poor of Boston. They can be made to see a life they didn't even know was possible for them. And I think that if anything comes out of tonight, one of the things we have to realize is that we've at least got to suffer as much as the South suffered. If it took them twenty or thirty years, we can't quit after two."

7

Responsibility and Freedom

EDWARD B. HANIFY

On the afternoon of June 9, 1976, at New England Life Hall, the closing speaker of the Bicentennial Forums was graciously introduced by Abram T. Collier:

"To conclude these Forums, we are fortunate this afternoon to have with us a leader of the Boston Bar. Boston has been proud of its many distinguished lawyers. In the eighteenth century, James Otis and John Adams were lawyers of renown, as was Daniel Webster in the nineteenth. In the 1950s it was a Boston lawyer, Joseph Welch, who on national television burst the overblown bubble that was Senator Joe McCarthy. And in the recent unpleasantness in Washington, most of the very few lawyers who escaped with reputations unscathed came from this city and cherished its traditions.

"Well-known Boston attorneys do not all fit the same mold. Our speaker, for example, has not held public office — nor does he fly his own airplane! He has, however, fulfilled the highest obligations of an attorney by representing a wide diversity of clients. Ed has enjoyed a fine reputation for thorough, painstaking, and effective work and for enjoying the challenges that come to him with each new and complex problem.

"Today he comes to us in a different capacity — not as a lawyer pleading another's case, but as a leading citizen of this community who has thought long and hard about this nation, its heritage, and

the responsibilities each of us must bear in the years that lie ahead.

"Son of a respected judge, our speaker graduated from college with the highest honors his college could bestow. At law school he compiled a brilliant record that led him to become associated with one of Boston's oldest and most reputable firms and with many other fine institutions as well. The positions and honors a citizen has received may call him to our attention, but it is the quality of his mind that holds our attention and commands our respect. Let me introduce you to a man whom I regard — in the best sense — as a Proper Bostonian."

ARTICLE XVIII of the Declaration of Rights of the Constitution of the Commonwealth of Massachusetts drafted by John Adams supplies the text of my remarks today on "Responsibility and Freedom." That Article reads in part as follows:

> A frequent recurrence to the fundamental principles of the constitution, and a constant adherence to those of piety, justice, moderation, temperance, industry, and frugality, are absolutely necessary to preserve the advantages of liberty, and to maintain a free government.

Having set forth this text, it may be well to define the terms "Responsibility" and "Freedom," and then state the basic thesis of my remarks.

I do not equate the term "Liberty" with "Freedom." Liberty denotes that set of external conditions which permits freedom of personal action. Freedom means the capacity of man, as a moral agent, to choose between right and wrong. Responsibility connotes the duty of the same moral agent to choose the right.

Both Freedom and Responsibility are concepts rooted in that view of human nature which holds that man is a created, rational, and social being.

This view of man, with his attributes of Freedom and Responsibility, constitutes the "Value System" or "Public Philosophy" which generated "The American Experiment." It was an experiment only in structures designed to conserve long-established values. Our Founding Fathers did not deem those values to be tentative and subject to test.

It is my submission that in contemporary America this philosophical foundation of our institutions is either ignored or contested. It is further imperiled because its sustaining nutrient civic virtues of Responsible Freedom are neglected or challenged. As we enter our next century, we are confronted with the desperate prospect of trying to maintain a governmental structure, a corpus of constitutional bone and sinew, while its soul or animating principle ebbs away.

One of the enduring memories of my boyhood is the annual Fourth of July civic celebration in my native city, Fall River. For youngsters of my generation, the Grand Army of the Republic was not represented by a gallant figure graven in stone and standing in lonely solemnity on the village green. A few survivors of the Union Army then marched with proud if halting step. After them came the veterans of the Spanish-American War. Then the vigorous young men returned from that relatively recent war "to make the world safe for Democracy." When the parade ended in an assembly in the park, by long-standing custom one of our own number, a youngster in grammar school or high school, then read the Declaration of Independence. The day was hot, the summer sun inexorable. The pursuit of happiness was an arduous and discouraging exercise to textile workers suffering a postwar depression in that industry. There was always silent attention, doubtless an unspoken hope for better days, as the young voice rang out the undying words:

> We hold these truths to be self-evident, that all men are created equal, that they are endowed by their Creator with certain unalienable Rights, that among these are Life, Liberty, and the pursuit of Happiness.

These words succinctly express a view of the nature of man on which Western civilization was created. Jefferson was not experimenting with principles. He stated his object in composing the Declaration was "not to find out new principles, or new arguments, never before thought of, not merely to say things that had never been said before; but to place before mankind the common sense of the subject in terms so plain and firm as to command their assent." He expressly acknowledged the influence in his formulation "of the elementary books of public right, as Aristotle, Cicero, Locke, Sidney." [1]

What do these familiar words of the Declaration mean? Are they an incantation rather than a political creed?

First of all, the Declaration asserts there exists a body of principles which can be called "truths." Yes, "self-evident truths," not pragmatic assumptions, not working hypotheses, but "truths." *"What is truth?"* asked Pilate on an unforgettable occasion, walking out before his question could be answered, and reflecting the speculative skepticism of his time. The Founding Fathers were not speculative skeptics. Clearly and cogently, they expressed a belief in the existence of objective reality with which the human mind can conform and thereby attain *Logical Truth;* and which the human voice or pen can proclaim which becomes *Moral Truth.* Because it has reality, Truth is capable of being translated into valid principles governing human actions and institutions.

Next, the Declaration asserts that man is a creature, with an endowment from his Creator, that endowment consisting of a grant of unalienable rights. Herein lies the antidote to the false pride of man, as well as the basis for his dignity. He is not self-sufficient. He cannot manipulate his fellow men. With them, he shares a *created* nature. However, the Creator of that nature has endowed it with unalienable rights. If man cannot treat his fellow men as his puppets or as cogs in his political, economic, or industrial machine, neither can he be

1. Becker, The Declaration of Independence 25 (1922).

rightfully subjected to such treatment by anyone or even a majority.

Finally, the unalienable rights with which the Creator has endowed his creature, man, are rights to Life, Liberty, and the pursuit of Happiness. These rights are the specific and differentiating marks of the rational soul. We do not speak of Liberty and the pursuit of Happiness in the case of atoms or animals. The arrow that is inexorably propelled to its target by the bow of the archer, the dog that reaches for a bone, responsive to physical laws and instinct, are *not* at Liberty in the pursuit of that intangible felicity we call "Happiness."

In these basic postulates, the Declaration of Independence enshrines what has been called a "natural law" philosophy — recognition of an infinite personal Creator, the source of man's unalienable rights and of moral obligation; principles of law and justice which transcend all human positive laws, and which have their basis in God; human nature properly understood in its created, rational, and social essence, as the measure in some sense of the immutable principles of right and wrong.[2]

This essential philosophy has been transmitted, in its various formulations and with some differences in interpretation, from Aristotle and Cicero, from Aquinas and Bracton, through Coke, Sidney, Locke, Blackstone, and Burke, to James Wilson, John Adams, and Thomas Jefferson, to name only some of our founders. Eminent scholars of our own day, including Mr. Justice Holmes's famous correspondent Dr. John C. H. Wu, have traced this golden thread through the civilizing centuries.[3] No one has stated the philosophical premises of our form of government more cogently in recent times than the late Walter Lippmann, who referred to the concept of "nat-

2. The Reverend John C. Ford, S.J., "The Natural Law and the 'Pursuit of Happiness,' " *Notre Dame Lawyer 429,* 26 (Spring 1951).

3. John C. H. Wu, "The Fountain of Justice, A Study in the Natural Law" (New York: Sheed and Ward, 1955). Benjamin Fletcher Wright, Jr., "American Interpretations of Natural Law" (Cambridge: Harvard University Press, 1931).

ural law" as the "public philosophy." Describing "The Forgotten Foundation" in 1938, he wrote: [4]

> [The authors of our liberties] said that man belonged to his Creator, and that since he was, therefore, an immortal soul, he possessed inalienable rights as a person which no power on earth had the right to violate . . . This is the forgotten foundation of democracy in the only sense in which democracy is truly valid and of liberty in the only sense in which it can hope to endure. The liberties we talk about defending today were established by men who took their conception of man from the great central religious tradition of Western civilization, and the liberties we inherit can almost certainly not survive the abandonment of that tradition.

Again in his famous address, "Education vs. Western Civilization," [5] Lippmann said:

> The institutions of the Western world were formed by men who learned to regard themselves as inviolable persons because they were rational and free. They meant by rational that they were capable of comprehending the moral order of the universe and their place in this moral order. They meant when they regarded themselves as free that within that order they had a personal moral responsibility to perform their duties and to exercise their corresponding rights. From this conception of the unity of mankind in a rational order the Western world has derived its conception of law — which is that all men and all communities of men and all authority among men are subject to law, and that the character of all particular laws is to be judged by whether they conform to or violate, approach or depart from, the rational order of the universe and of man's nature . . . In this tradition our world was made. By this tradition it must live. Without this tradition our world, like a tree cut off from its roots in the soil, must die and be replaced by alien and barbarous things . . .

What chance would the plain language and underlying principles of the Declaration of Independence have today to achieve a consensus among the leaders of public opinion, the

---

4. "The Forgotten Foundation," Today and Tomorrow, December 17, 1938, in *The Essential Lippmann* (1963).
5. "Education vs. Western Civilization," *The American Scholar* X (1941), 184.

molders of American thought, the educators of the young, and indeed the general American electorate?

One can readily hear the probable chorus of dissent. Some would say, "Let us not talk of self-evident truths. That involves a commitment to a philosophical system of realism. Let us rather proceed on the basis of working hypotheses."

Others would find the unequivocal assertion of a right to life troublesome, and would suggest a qualification drawn from recent opinions of the United States Supreme Court so that the Declaration would read that the Right to Life is the unalienable right of only those human beings who have the capacity for meaningful life.

Still others would find the postulate of creaturehood for man, and Creatorship for God, and the references in the Declaration to "Nature's God" and the "Supreme Judge of the World" an unacceptable effort to impose the personal religious convictions of the authors upon the generality of mankind.

The Humanist Manifesto of 1933 and the Humanist Manifesto II of 1973 were subscribed to by important molders of both world and American public opinion. The 1973 document bore the signatures of the leaders or chief executives of some of the most influential organizations of our time.

The influence of these Manifestos on contemporary mores and jurisprudence has been marked. Both express views of God and man which sharply diverge from the Declaration's. Further, the Humanist Manifesto of 1973 states:

> As in 1933 humanists still believe that traditional theism, especially faith in the prayer-hearing God, assumed to love and care for persons, to hear and understand their prayers, and to be able to do something about them is an unproved and outmoded faith.[6]

The signers of the Declaration of Independence, however, explicitly adhered to this so-called "unproved and outmoded faith": They appealed to "The Supreme Judge of the World for

6. The *New York Times*, August 26, 1973, "Human Manifesto Offers Survival Policy."

the rectitude of *their* intentions." For the support of this Declaration, they expressed "firm reliance on the Protection of Divine Providence."

In the Constitution of the Commonwealth of Massachusetts, our own founders expressly acknowledge in its Preamble, "The goodness of the great Legislator of the universe in affording us in the course of His Providence," an opportunity to enter into that solemn compact, and devoutly implored "His direction in so interesting a design" for self-government.

In this Bicentennial year, we should face the reality that we no longer have a general consensus on the public philosophy from which our institutions derived their origin and sustenance. It is not that the foundation is merely forgotten, it is that it is consciously not accepted by, or acceptable to, a substantial number of our contemporaries. The issue confronting the nation as she enters her third century is whether her governmental institutions will endure when uprooted from the basic concept of man's essential nature which originally nourished them.

We can scarcely expect to survive on lip service to ideals which we no longer consider valid. As one who subscribes frankly to the original thesis, I submit no course is more exigent than a speedy return to the truths of our philosophical origins, to the civic virtues which were deemed by our forefathers to be indispensable to the survival of our system of government, and to the strengthening of those essential nongovernmental resources which nourished and transmitted those basic virtues.

"Liberty," said Woodrow Wilson, "is the privilege of maturity, of self-mastery, and a thoughtful care for righteous dealing." The framers of the government of this Commonwealth were equally clear that its viability depended upon the existence of a responsible citizenry. Nor did they leave responsibility undefined or at large. They categorized those specific qualities of responsible freedom which they deemed essential.

They raised them to the dignity of solemn constitutional enumeration. Listen again to these words of admonition in Article XVIII of the Declaration of Rights of the Constitution of this Commonwealth:

> A frequent recurrence to the fundamental principles of the constitution, and a constant adherence to those of piety, justice, moderation, temperance, industry, and frugality, are absolutely necessary to preserve the advantages of liberty, and to maintain a free government. The people ought, consequently, to have a particular attention to all those principles, in the choice of their officers and representatives: and they have a right to require of their lawgivers and magistrates, an exact and constant observance of them, in the formation and execution of the laws necessary for the good administration of the commonwealth.

Again, Section 30 of Chapter 71 of the Massachusetts General Laws, a statute which went on our books in 1789, reads as follows:

> The president, professors, and tutors of the university at Cambridge and of the several colleges, all preceptors and teachers of academies and all other instructors of youth shall exert their best endeavors to impress on the minds of children and youth committed to their care and instruction the principles of piety and justice and a sacred regard for truth, love of their country, humanity and universal benevolence, sobriety, industry and frugality, chastity, moderation and temperance, and those other virtues which are the ornament of human society and the basis upon which a republican constitution is founded; and they shall endeavor to lead their pupils, as their ages and capacities will admit, into a clear understanding of the tendency of the above mentioned virtues to preserve and perfect a republican constitution and secure the blessings of liberty as well as to promote their future happiness, and also to point out to them the evil tendency of the opposite vices.

Piety, Justice, Truthfulness, Patriotism, Humanity, Benevolence, Sobriety, Industry, Frugality, Chastity, Moderation, and Temperance!

What is the attitude of contemporary society to these qualities? In the slang of the day would they be referred to as "square" or "corny"? In the semantics of the sophisticated, would their constitutional description be considered simplistic and old-fashioned rhetoric with unhappy "judgmental" or "pejorative" connotations? Is it not always the bigoted dunderhead on the "family" TV program who protests his liberal son-in-law's obscene blasphemy of the Deity to the canned laughter of the audience? On the tube that holds Americans either enthralled or in thralldom are not these constitutional virtues often turned into unlovely caricatures, "the lilies and languors of virtue" to be contrasted with the "raptures and roses of vice"? Yet, the very sagacious men who drafted the Constitution of this Commonwealth deemed these qualities "absolutely necessary to preserve the advantages of liberty and to maintain a free government." In short, they considered these private virtues to be affected with a public interest. They represented the habitual choice of right rather than wrong. They were the indicia of freedom with responsibility.

This emphasis by our founders on the social necessity of norms of responsible conduct is not obsolete. The best thinkers in modern jurisprudence have echoed the very same views. The distinguished British jurist, the honorable Sir Patrick Devlin, in his memorable Maccabaean Lecture on Jurisprudence, "The Enforcement of Morals," [7] put the matter very plainly:

> If men and women try to create a society in which there is no fundamental agreement about good and evil they will fail; if having based it on agreement, the agreement goes, the society will disintegrate. For society is not something that is kept together physically; it is held by the invisible bonds of common thought . . . A common morality is part of the bondage. The bondage is part of the price of society; and mankind, which needs society, must pay its price.

7. Maccabaean Lecture in Jurisprudence, "The Enforcement of Morals," by the Hon. Sir Patrick Devlin, read March 18, 1959, Proceedings of the British Academy.

You will recall that in its litany of the essential attributes of the responsible citizen, the Constitution of this Commonwealth, adopted in 1780, expressly mentioned the quality of "*Moderation.*"

In 1942 the Commonwealth of Massachusetts observed, with appropriate ceremonies, the two hundred and fiftieth anniversary of its Supreme Judicial Court — the oldest tribunal of its kind in the nation. On that occasion that profound jurist Learned Hand of New York made a memorable address. He had discussed the role of the judiciary in preserving the fundamental principles of equity and fair play which the Constitution of the United States enshrines. He then turned to a consideration of the future fate of those principles and made this prophetic utterance:

> What will be left of those principles [of justice]? I do not know whether they will serve only as counsels; but this much I think I do know — that a society so riven that the spirit of moderation is gone, no court can save; that a society where that spirit flourishes, no court need save; that in a society which evades its responsibility by thrusting upon courts the nurture of that spirit, that spirit in the end will perish. What is the spirit of moderation? It is the temper which does not press partisan advantage to the bitter end, which can understand and will respect the other side, which feels a unity between all citizens — real and not the factitious product of propaganda — which recognizes their common fate and their common aspirations — in a word, which has faith in the sacredness of the individual. Men must take that temper and that faith with them into the field, into the marketplace, into the factory, into the council room, into their homes; they cannot be imposed; they must be lived. Words will not express them; arguments will not clarify them; decisions will not maintain them. They are the fruit of the wisdom that comes of trial and a pure heart.[8]

Do not current events in our own community prove the wisdom of those words of Judge Hand?

8. Address by the Hon. Learned Hand at a banquet celebrating the 250th anniversary of the Founding of the Supreme Judicial Court, Boston, Massachusetts, November 21, 1942.

A society so riven that the spirit of moderation is gone, no court can save.

A society where that spirit flourishes, no court need save.

In a society which evades its responsibility by thrusting upon courts the nurture of that spirit, that spirit in the end will perish.

An interesting exchange of correspondence took place in 1857 between Henry S. Randall, the biographer of Thomas Jefferson, and Thomas Babington Macaulay, the English author and statesman. Macaulay foresaw periods of social unrest and economic distress in the United States. He had no confidence that the majority of the people would have sufficient patience and forbearance to suffer through these times of anguish. He believed the American Constitution was "all sail and no anchor" because it would not be able to restrain the ensuing violent public reaction. So he wrote: [9]

Either some Caesar or Napoleon will seize the reins of government with a strong hand, or your Republic will be as fearfully plundered and laid waste by barbarians in the 20th Century as the Roman Empire was in the fifth, with this difference, that the Huns and Vandals who ravaged the Roman Empire came from without, and that your Huns and Vandals will have been engendered within your own country by your own institutions.

If Macaulay were to survey the current scene with its violent crime, senseless brutality and vandalism, its guns and its bombs, its sexual promiscuity, perversion, and pornography, its shoplifting and bag-snatching, its widespread theft and burglary, its marital infidelity, broken homes, deserted children, its aborted unborn, its terrified aged, its alcoholism, drug culture, and highway carnage, he would doubtless say:

Your Huns and Vandals are here, in core city and affluent suburb alike. The private virtues of responsible citizenship on which your founders expressly relied in establishing the rule of the people have

9. The Constitution of the United States, James M. Beck, Appendix IV.

been substantially destroyed. Your institutions consequently have no operative checks on these violent assaults. You await the dictator who will insure that you walk safely on your streets, feel secure in your homes, avert confiscation of your savings, and who may suspend in the process your vaunted personal liberties. For freedom requires responsibility — and you do not have it.

We would not readily accept Macaulay's "I told you so." We would insist that there is still a great reservoir of responsible character in our citizenry. However, we would be purblind if we did not recognize the warning signs.

To avert disaster, we do need a profound change in the direction of our contemporary mores and fresh insight into our original public philosophy. The United States cannot drift into a new century as a society without norms to guide responsible action. These norms must be reintroduced with conviction and reinforced by education in values in home and school.

What stands in the way of reenergizing responsible freedom through a fresh insistence on the norms or values that make it a reality?

First, there is the all too prevalent state of mind that treats responsibility as The Case of the Missing Person. Norms of conduct are not applied to individuals. Structures are always to blame for our ills. Society is at fault. Capital Letter Abstractions are culpable. The System is the criminal. Individuals are never failing the community, the community is always failing the individual. Of course, there are abhorrent environments which are conducive to the development of antisocial attitudes. However, with all due regard for the existence of actual mental aberrations deranging the individual intellect or overpowering the will, with all proper allowance for the existence of social conditions that produce temptations to crime and immorality, there is no basis upon which our society can operate except the principle that in the generality of cases, man is capable of making a choice between right and wrong

145

and accountable for that choice.[10] The surest way to increase the number of Macaulay's Huns and Vandals in our midst is to assume that they are devoid of any personal accountability because their conduct is always predetermined by social, economic, or psychological influences utterly beyond their control. There is such a thing in the objective order as "Evil" or "Iniquity." It is in the nature of man's freedom that he can choose it. The choice is made by individuals, rich and poor, deprived and fortunate. Let us not, as a matter of course, transfer the responsibility of the individual for that choice to a collectivity.

The next obstacle frequently interposed to our reemphasis of norms for responsible social conduct is the frequent outcry that in a pluralistic society we must be careful not to impose our religious or moral standards on others. Let us be wary of the misapplication of a reasonable principle of religious freedom so that in the area of moral standards, it becomes a shelter for the equivocal, an excuse for the indifferent, and a deterrent to the well disposed. When we defend the concept of man's rational, social, and created nature on which the nation was founded, we are not trying to force anyone else to adopt an article of a particular religious Faith.

The view of our fathers as to man's rights, freedom, and responsibility was not a tenet of any particular religious creed. It was not exclusively Catholic or Protestant or Jewish. It was the fruit of the Judeo-Christian tradition permeating Western civilization. Obviously, the American ideal has moral and religious elements, for the nation was not conceived in a moral or religious vacuum. When the United States Constitution forbade laws respecting an establishment of religion, it did not thereby establish a system of nonstandards as the country's official national Irreligion. We would be cowards fleeing before

10. "The Philosophy of Responsibility," address of Bishop (now Cardinal) John J. Wright at the April 16, 1959, Isaiah Thomas Award Dinner in Worcester, Massachusetts.

a slogan if we let this film of dust distract us from an effort to preserve the virtues of the reponsible free man enumerated in the Constitution of this Commonwealth against the onslaught of those who from greed or malignity would prefer to have the antithetical vices become the norms of human conduct. If we do not insist that man's rationality remain in control of his animality, those who place his rationality in bondage to his animality will prevail.

If slogans and shibboleths do not deter us from a vigorous effort to reintroduce or at least reemphasize norms of responsible conduct in American life, what means do we have at hand for the practical accomplishment of the ideal of responsible freedom? The inevitable answer is the family and the school.

I am generally aware of the processes traumatically affecting family life today which Talcott Parsons has described as the "disorganization of transition." However, has any one of us seen any credible evidence that the family will not or should not remain for the foreseeable future the primary social unit, or that the commune can take its place as the moral, biological, and psychological nexus of society. If this is so, is there any escape from the sociologist Michael Novak's recent position [11] that young people today who make a loving commitment to each other in marriage and choose to have a family are performing an act of intelligence and courage which had the quality of civic virtue? These newly created family units, which should have the maximum support of enlightened public policy, are the best hope the nation has of preserving and transmitting the values and norms of responsible freedom to generations yet to be. They are small craft launched on perilous seas; but their cargo is nothing less precious than the future of the American dream.

I remember years ago during my World War II service, trudging around a metropolitan area, searching for a place for

11. Michael Novak, "The Family out of Favor," *Harper's*, April 1976.

a young family only to meet the discouraging sign or read the sour advertisement: "No children or pets." Today, in some circles children have moved down below "pets" in the priority of social protection. If we are to frame an enlightened public policy for the American family as Ambassador Moynihan has suggested, I should like to see it contain a Bill of Rights for Children, born and unborn, so that they are not treated as "products of conception," emerging, if permitted, from a "nine-month disease known as pregnancy," but as the most welcome, the most hopeful, the most innocent of humankind.

A final and necessarily brief word about the role of education, public and private, in the inculcation of the ethical norms of responsible freedom. It is well known that professional and graduate schools are now offering courses, sometimes mandatory, dealing with the ethical norms of business or the professions. The awareness of the need to emphasize norms of responsible conduct at this ultimate point in the educational process should highlight the even more pressing reason for kindred, if more basic, normative formulation in those prior stages of public and private education which involve the generality of our young people. To those who suggest that young people should discover standards of ethical conduct on their own, the answer is that those standards are part of their civilized inheritance. They have a right to know them. To those who suggest that the standards of private virtue which characterize responsible freedom are so clothed in antiquated expression and connotation that they "turn young people off" the answer is clear: If these values really invoke profound adult conviction, then their transmission through palatable pedagogy is a matter of technique which should not be impossible for a civilization that can make vice alluring, and even glamorize deodorants, detergents, and cathartics.

Men of our generation, like those of any generation, may be likened to dwarfs seated on the shoulders of giants as we borrow the vision and stature of men of many past centuries.

From that vantage point, we see beyond the present unhappy scene. We have the great vistas of centuries of civilized human action to contemplate, where men have directed blows at the painted face of falsehood and deceit, written great poems, composed majestic music, faced with humility and honest labor each day with its petty round of irritating concerns and duties, performed countless unremembered acts of kindness and love, fought valiantly, shed their blood for selfless aims, dethroned tyrants, toppled dictators, lived nobly and died grandly — all in conformity with the ideals of responsible freedom enshrined in our basic philosophy. To say that we cannot unfold this panorama of man's essential dignity for young people to whom life is still a fresh adventure, or elicit their enthusiasm for and devotion to these ideals, is an awful confession either of our own lack of conviction or our own impoverished advocacy. We have abundant teaching aids.

To quote Woodrow Wilson: "I have found more true politics in the poets of the English-speaking race," he said, "than I have ever found in all the treatises on political science." Perhaps as he suggested, both for young and old, a few lines of Tennyson may capture the spirit of our institutions as well as all the textbooks on government.

> A nation still, the rulers and the ruled.
> Some sense of duty, something of a faith,
> Some reverence for the laws ourselves have made,
> Some patient force to change them when we will,
> Some civic manhood firm against the crowd.

This is the fair form in which we hold out the concept and reality of responsible freedom to those who must transmit that ideal unimpaired and unimperiled to their posterity.

149

Questions and Discussion

Hanify's address illumined a broad spectrum of issues, values, and beliefs, and the questions and discussion that followed that afternoon and evening dramatically showed how far we have drifted from that "consensus among the leaders of public opinion, the molders of American thought," on which the Republic had been founded.

Many of the questions raised at the end of the address showed widespread interest among his listeners in this issue. Do the peoples of Western Europe subscribe to the beliefs on which the American government was based? How can to-day's public leaders "believe," in the face of universal cynicism and venality? Are the classic civic virtues possible in a society that stresses collective rather than individual responsibility? What can our leaders do to restore the lost consensus? What has created our apathy and indifference? What forces have undermined our basic civic beliefs and the practice of our civic virtues? In a sense these were less questions than echoes of agreement and sympathetic reenforcement of what the speaker had said.

But the discussion at the Parkman House that evening took a different turn. One of the guests, an executive of a local television station, set its principal topic and direction by asking what is good for the country in terms of the media, specifically what policy should television follow. Many stations, he said, broadcast twenty or even twenty-four hours a day, and since there is never enough high-quality material to fill that much time, much of the content is mediocre to poor. Would it be better for the country to limit the broadcasting hours to as few as eight per day, and use only the best material we have.

Hanify agreed enthusiastically with this suggestion, but an ebullient young news analyst from another Boston television station took strong exception. If people sit passively before the tube all hours of the day or night — and that can be better than some other things they might do — it is the broadcaster's responsibility to give them something to make them more than vegetables. There are plenty of people in television with ideas worth listening to. In New York, with cable-TV, you can watch pornography, so why in Boston can't you watch culture at three in the morning? Put on three hours of right-wingers, or left-wingers, or right-to-lifers, or any other group that has real beliefs and something they urgently want to say, and put them on any hour of the day or night.

Several of the discussants felt that some of our TV stations don't make any effort to broadcast anything except the liberal-establishment views they hold themselves and which they know will sell. We need controversy, and challenge, and alternative views, they say — all the stuff they can't use on the six o'clock news or sell to their advertisers. Radio has a lot of this, but TV doesn't dare — "prison reform, leftist opinions and rightist; gay stuff, Lesbian stuff, Feminist stuff — even word stuff like Charles Dickens and Shakespeare and the Latin poets you would like to have on TV."

At this point a discussant who had recently sat on the Population Commission cited statements made in a meeting of that body showing how the commission used the media to disseminate its doctrines. She added that the women's movement is a creation of the media, and the civil rights movement, and so were most of the leaders in both. To which a TV commentator agreed, and added that the women on the Boston TV stations are all liberals — feminists, pro-abortion, pro-E.R.A., and so on. And it should be considered the duty of these stations to hire others to give equal representation to the opposite views, but none of them does.

"The media are the most perfect device yet invented for the dissemination of ideas and information, and the terrible thing is that they are out of balance — and not that some stations are on twenty-four hours a day while some are on less."

Hanify tried to bring the discussion back to his own main

point. "The whole trend of the media is against my kind of standards, against the case I make for a natural moral law, that the Deity had a plan for the whole universe, and promulgated for man the natural moral law by giving him a rational faculty through which he could decide by conscience what is right and what is wrong. I look at Maude, or at Archie Bunker, and I see nothing but a pervasive effort by the media to erode any respect for the idea of right and wrong as these can be discovered through man's basic nature. You see Archie Bunker and his son-in-law, and Bunker is protesting. Bunker is the protagonist of everything bigoted, narrow, and absolutely absurd. And yet *he* is made the protagonist of the case against blasphemy! And Maude, a sophisticate, makes the case for abortion. So you can see why I feel that the media in this country are conditioned against absolute standards of morality. In my view what is right is what is in conformity with man's nature, rational, social, and created — and what is wrong is what is against it. The media don't believe in any such standards, as far as I can see, and indeed are making a deliberate effort to erode them. I would like to hear anyone who wishes to defend the opposite position."

While none of the discussants specifically defended the opposite position as a whole, the invitation brought out a number of interesting points of view. One TV man agreed that the media have an ideological bias against the traditional moral philosophy because media people do not represent the population as a whole, but only a particular segment of it: "There is not one anchorman in New York, and not one in Boston, who is anything but a Left-Liberal." Another added that the standard attitudes and beliefs for these people are set by the *New York Times* and the Washington *Post*. Still another, who spoke not as a media insider but simply as a viewer, felt that the views expressed by the media in no sense reflected a conspiracy by liberals or by anyone else, but simply reflected their view of what sells. He believes that they are guided by no ideology whatsoever, but simply by the profit motive.

One speaker raised the charge that on controversial issues the media sometimes stacked the cards on one side or the other, and he cited his own extensive experience as evidence. Having spoken on television against abortion some 200 times, he found it not infrequent for a panel to consist of three or four in favor to one against, and that he had sometimes not been told there would be a panel but only a single speaker on the other side, and sometimes none at all. He said he had received assurances from major networks, newspapers, news magazines, and general magazines that as a matter of policy they would not print anything against abortion. "If that is not conspiracy," he concluded, "I don't know what conspiracy is."

This testimony was followed by that from a *Time* magazine correspondent who had been subjected to the same technique of loading an interview, though she had been the "liberal" and the interviewer the "conservative." The topic of discussion, which was announced only after the discussion was under way, was "How *Time* Magazine Sensationalizes the News," and she found herself one against four. She concluded that she did not think loading the discussion was so much a matter of ideology as of making the program as lively and entertaining as possible. And she quoted the moderator's opening remark, "If you picked up a table and threw it at me, that would really make the point. No holds barred!"

This speaker went on to say that she saw the media as a reflection of our society, not usually as a leader of it. She felt that the media are often behind the society and in need of catching up. She then commented that she had been most struck in the afternoon's address by Hanify's statement about the breakup of the consensus, and herself thought that this reflected many changes in the last two hundred years — that we have become a kind of "Global Village," in which people know more about each other than ever before, and all experience things at the same time, with knowledge of each other through the media. "New questions have been raised, new conditions introduced, and I find people earnestly trying to deal with them, and seeking the truths you are talking about, only they don't yet know where they are going to come out."

At this point another member of the group, a historian, tried hard to move the discussion away from the media on to what he felt was a more central — or at least an equally important — aspect of Hanify's subject. The media, and the commercialization of ideas, he said, were only a fraction of what Hanify had talked about. He agreed with Hanify that a certain tacit moral code underlay the Declaration of Independence and the Constitution, but that something else also lay at the core of civic virtue, and that was the institution of the family. And in the family as well as in politics and business, the question arises, in these days of broken consensus, how shall we find the ground of common civic virtue? When groups diverge and each feels it possesses the truth, how shall we find some common ground? Perhaps it can be some minimum on which all can agree, rather than some idealistic maximum. Perhaps we should not try to define *the* right way for families to live, but to find some common good all could agree on and accept.

"To make a start, I think we would all agree that it is extraordinarily hard to be a parent in America today. In a way this is a society hostile to those who are trying to bring up children. I suspect that most of those virtues you read out from the Massachusetts Constitution are not being taught by most parents to their children in the Commonwealth today. And since there is no longer any consensus outside the family, teaching these virtues is not enough anyway.

"Where then can we look for a common ground? For one thing, I think we would all agree that every head of a family who wants to go out and work should be able to bring home a living wage. We know from all kinds of studies, and from experience, that bringing home a living wage is an enormous help to a family raising children. Yet ours is not now a society that makes this possible. Why then could it not be a universally accepted minimum goal that this is one of the things we want to accomplish? We could then ask what, as a society, we could do to make this possible. Here is a minimum goal no one would challenge. And it is widely believed and probably demonstrable that he who eats is less eager to destroy society than he who hungers. Yet in about half the land area of the city of Boston — in South Boston, Roxbury, and parts of Dorchester and Jamaica Plain — thousands of our fellow Bostonians are trying to form families, are working but are not bringing home a living wage. That is an essential issue we should all agree on, and it is of the greatest urgency."

Hanify agreed, and added that one of the most horrible of recent statistics was that in Chicago about 40 percent of black males between seventeen and twenty-five are unemployed — an attack on family life which did not occur in Ben Franklin's day. "Yet there is a difference between social issues and moral questions which go to the root of things. Murder, adultery, theft, the Ten Commandments — put those on one side. Don't ask me to defend the Ten Commandments on the basis of whether I believe in fair share or the graduated income tax. We can argue questions of means to social ends. But if I happen to be against stealing, or murder, or abortion, that doesn't mean I am pro-fair share or anti-fair share. These are issues of a different order."

And finally the historian, once more in search of a synthesis, cited three facts: First, the Commonwealth of Massachusetts is historically interesting because since its first census, on which Thomas Malthus drew in his book, *On Population*, in 1798, the fertility rate has been steadily declining. Second, around 1850 the Massachusetts population became dominantly Catholic. And third, throughout the country blacks and whites, rural and urban, immigrants included, have been restricting the size of families from the eighteenth century to the present day, except for the period after World War II. No one knows why this is true; we can only say that it has in fact happened.

So it seems no historical accident that the issue of abortion and birth control should surface at the present time. This issue merely reveals and describes the long-term behavior of millions of people, and it is inevitable that it should have its opponents as well as its proponents. Indeed, it could be thought of as only one more aspect of the broken consensus.

But we cannot deny these things. We cannot go backward, however comfortable a simpler past may seem to us today. If our work is in fragments, there is only one way we can save it. We must put it together again out of those fragments, not as we wish they were, but as they are.

Epilogue

ABRAM T. COLLIER

IT IS with some reluctance that we bring to a close these Bicentennial Forums. In the last eighteen months we have been privileged to hear from a dozen eminent thinkers. They have told us of the American Experiment and the American Prospect. They have pointed out that while our past has made us what we are, what we are is also determined by what we expect to be.

The American Prospect cannot be divined, for only the Divinity can perceive the future. Nonetheless, as time-binding creatures, we reach out to the future through such fine and perceptive minds as have graced our celebration.

I would like, if I may, to close these gatherings by quoting from a resident of this Commonwealth, who was trained in the law but is celebrated as a poet and playwright. I would like to read a few portions of one of Archibald MacLeish's better-known poems, called *America was Promises*. As I read, you should keep in mind the fact it was *written some thirty-seven years ago*, before World War II, and before its horrors became known. In this poem, MacLeish wrote:

> America was always promises.
> From the first voyage and the first ship
>   there were promises . . .
> America was promises — to whom?

157

Jefferson knew:
Declared it before God and before history:
Declares it still in the remembering tomb . . .
It was Man the promise contemplated.
The times had chosen Man: no other . . .
It was Man who had been promised: who should have.
Man was to ride from the Tidewater: over the Gap:
West and South with the water: taking the book with him:
Taking the wheat seed . . .
Building liberty a farmyard wide . . .
Old Man Adams knew. He told us . . .
"The first want of every man was his dinner:
The second his girl" . . .
Enlightened selfishness gave lasting light.
Winners bred grandsons: losers only bred . . .
The Aristocracy of Wealth and Talents
Turned its talents into wealth and lost them . . .
Tom Paine knew.
Tom Paine knew the People.
The promises were spoken to the People . . .
Whatever was truly built the People had built it.
Whatever was taken down they had taken down . . .
The People had the Promises: they'd keep them.
They waited their time in the world . . .
When the time came they would speak and the rest
    would listen.
And the time came and the People did not speak . . .
We do not ask for Truth now from John Adams.
We do not ask for Tongues from Thomas Jefferson.
We do not ask for Justice from Tom Paine.
We ask for answers.
And there is an answer.
There is Spain Austria Poland China Bohemia.
There are dead men in the pits in all those countries.
Their mouths are silent but they speak. They say
"The promises are theirs who take them" . . .
Listen! You have heard these words. Believe it!
Believe the promises are theirs who take them . . .
Believe unless we take them for ourselves
Others will take them for the use of others . . .
Men not Man: People not the People . . .

America is promises to
Take!
America is promises to
Us
To take them
Brutally
With love but
Take them.
Oh, believe this!

MacLeish still speaks for us all. As Americans we continue to vibrate to the idea that America is promises, promises that can only be fulfilled in the future. We also recognize that our future is ours, *if* we take it, *if* we plan for it, *if* we work hard enough for it.